Latina Leadership Institute
From vision to Reality 20th Anniversary
1999 - 2019

Tomás Alberto Ávila

© 2019 by Tomás Alberto Ávila. All Rights Reserved. All rights reserved. Except as permitted under the United States Copyright act of 1976, no part of this publication may be reproduced or distributed or by any means or stored in a database or retrieval system without the prior written of the publisher.

First Printing December 2019

Published by
Milenio Latino Institute, Inc.
Providence, Rhode Island
tavila@mileniolatinoinstitute.org

Library of Congress Catalog Card Number: Pending

ISBN 978-1-928810-48-3

Printed in the United Stated of America.

Table of Contents

In Celebration of the 100th Anniversary of the Nineteenth Amendment to the United States Constitution and the Success of the Latina Leadership Institute 11

Latinas Outreach Project in the Rhode Island Political Process 15

    INTRODUCTION 15
    MISSION 15
    OBJECTIVES 15
    PROJECT LEADERSHIP... 16
        Margarita Guedes...16
        Melba DePeña 16
        Eva Hulse-Avila 16
        Betty Bernal 16
        Delia Rodriguez-Masjoan...16

Latinas @ a Crossroad: Our Political Empowerment 17

    Honoring the Past, Celebrating the Present & Imagining the Future 17
        Keynote Speaker 17
        Venue 17
        Potential Sponsors 17
        The Pride of Our Century 18

Congressional Resolution Designating the Month of March "Women's History Month" 19

Timeline of Key Events in the American Women's Rights Movement 20

    THE DECLARATION OF SENTIMENTS 27
        Seneca Falls, New York, 1848.......................................27
        Sentiments..27
        Resolutions...30
        Amendment XIX 32

Destino 2002: Latina Political Empowerment Project...........33

    CREATED BY MELBA DEPEÑA AND TOMÁS ÁVILA....................33
        The Need 33

The Goal *34*
DESTINO 2002: LATINA POLITICAL EMPOWERMENT PROJECT 34
    The Objectives *34*
    The Program *35*
  CONFERENCE: LATINAS AT A CROSS ROAD 36
  PROPOSED CALENDAR OF EVENTS FOR LATINA POLITICAL INSTITUTE 36
    August 26, 2000 .... *36*
    September 2000 .... *36*
    October 2000 .... *37*
    November 2000 .... *37*
    December 2000 .... *37*
    January 2001 .... *37*

2002 The Rhode Island Latino Civic Fund (RILCF) Established **45**

2003 Rhode Island Foundation Latina Leadership Institute Letter of Intent **46**

  MELBA DEPENA & DELIA RODRIGUEZ MASJOAN 46
    February 26, 2003 .... *46*

2003 Latina Leadership Institute **48**

  ORGANIZATION MISSION STATEMENT 48
  PROJECT DESCRIPTION 48
  THE NEED 49
  THE GOAL 49
  THE OBJECTIVES 50
  PRESS RELEASE 50
  2003 LLI GRADUATES 52
  30 **LATINAS GRADUATE FROM THE LATINA LEADERSHIP INSTITUTE** 53

Latina Leadership Institute 2005 Restructuring **56**

  2005 PROGRAM SCHEDULE 57
  PROGRAM DESCRIPTION 58
    Program Purposes and Goals *58*
    Vision *59*
    Mission *59*

Purpose *59*
AMONG LATINA LEADERSHIP INSTITUTE'S LONG-TERM GOALS ARE THE FOLLOWING: 60
   Target Population *60*
   The Leadership Program *61*
  COMPONENTS 61
   Skills-Building Seminars *62*
  LATINA LEADERSHIP INSTITUTE COMPONENTS 62
   Skills-Building Seminars *62*
   Committees and Task Forces *62*
   Other Structured Activities *63*
   Community Project *63*
   Associate Meetings *63*
   Supplemental Activities *63*

PROGRAM STRUCTURE 65
   Week 1: General Introduction *65*
   Week 2: Getting to know our Community *65*
   Week 3: Leadership Theory *65*
   Week 4: Communication Skills *66*
   Week 5: Public Policy *67*
   Week 6: Grassroots Leadership and Activism *67*
   Week 7. Introduction to Boards & Commissions *67*
   Week 8: Working With the Media *68*
  CAMPAIGN TRAINING WORKSHOP AGENDA 69

2005 APPLICATION INFORMATION 73
  CAMPAIGN TRAINING APPLICATION 84
  CAMPAIGN ACTIVITIES EXTENSIVE SOME LITTLE NONE .. 85
  MARKETING 86
   Press Release *86*

Invitation Letter 89
  Latina Leadership Institute Presenters Letter *90*

Reference 91

The Rhode Island Latino Civic Fund 93
  CHALLENGES AND OPPORTUNITIES 94

Latina Leadership Class Puts Emphasis On Social Advocacy, Political Involvement 97

Latina Institute Graduates 17 Leaders 99

   THE PROGRAM IS AIMED AT YOUNG WOMEN WHO HAVE A BACKGROUND IN PUBLIC SERVICE, EDUCATION AND GOVERNMENT. 99
- *Yolanda Baez* *100*
- *Evelyn Castillo* *100*
- *Martha Cedeño* *100*
- *Rosa Q. Crowley* *100*
- *Cynthia DeJesus* *100*
- *Irisonixa Diaz* *100*
- *Diana Figueroa* *100*
- *Judelkys García* *100*
- *Alma Guzmán* *100*
- *Judith Koegler* *100*
- *Katia Lugo* *100*
- *Olinda Matos* *100*
- *Vivian Moreno* *100*
- *Sonja Ogando* *100*
- *Patricia Patterson* *100*
- *Rosemary Raygada* *100*
- *Silvia Reyes.* *100*

2006 LLI 101

LLI 2007 102

   CONGRATULATIONS TO OBED PAPP LLI 2007 102

LLI 2008 103

   CONGRATULATIONS TO CARMEN DIAZ-JUSINO LLI 2008.. 103

2009 LLI 104

2010 LLI 106

2011 LLI 107

   INSTITUTO DE LIDERAZGO CELEBRA GRADUACIÓN DE SU CLASE 2011 111
- *Las graduandas fueron:* *112*
- *Lissette Carmona* *112*
- *Paula Choquette* *112*

    Marcia De Jesús *112*
    Josefina Días. *112*
    Miguelina Domínguez *112*
    Mélida Espinal *112*
    Elizabeth Fernández *112*
    Magali García. *112*
    Lissette Guzmán *112*
    Mercy Parada *112*
    Karina Peláez *112*
    Aura Sánchez *112*
    Iris Silva. *112*
    Magira Valentiner. *112*
    Natalia Zapata *112*
Forman parte también del Comité Coordinador del Programa de Líderes Latinas: 114
    Doris Blanchard *114*
    Grace González. *114*
    Osmary Rodríguez *114*
    Norelys Consuegra *114*
    Francia Pacheco *114*
    Vianela Núñez. *114*

2013 LLI **116**

2014 LLI **124**

    New LLI Coordinator Norelys Consuegra 124
        Norelys R. Consuegra *125*
    House Resolution Extending Congratulations 126

2015 LLI **147**

2016 LLI **173**

    A New Dawn for the Rhode Island Latina Leadership Institute (LLI) 173
    Roger Williams University School of Continuing Studies partners with Rhode Island Latino Civic Fund *173*
    Comments *177*

Adriana Dawson **178**

Roger Williams University School of Continuing Studies partners with Rhode Island Latino Civic Fund **180**

2017 LLI **183**

Arts for Education Fundraiser **199**

2018 LLI **202**

   THANK SECRETARY OF STATE NELLIE M. GORBEA 203
   LLI ALUMNI AWARD RECIPIENTS: 204
      Julia Gutierrez, LLI 13 .... *204*
      Maria Rivera, LLI 14 .... *204*
      Andrea Gomez, LLI 15 .... *204*
      Dorca Paulino, LLI 17 .... *204*
   12 GRADUATE FROM LATINA LEADERSHIP INSTITUTE 253
      The Institute *254*
      The Graduates are Listed Below *254*

LLI has Gone International **255**

   HOW TO EXPRESS MY SINCERE APPRECIATION 259

Melinda Lopez Appointed Director **263**

Norelys R. Consuegra **265**

Alumni **266**

   SABINA MATOS 267
   9 THINGS TO KNOW ABOUT R.I. SEN.-ELECT SANDRA CANO'S
   POLITICS, POLICIES 269
      1. Schooling *269*
      2. Rebuilding Rhode Island's crumbling schools *270*
      3. Empowering women *270*
      4. Keep the PawSox in Pawtucket? *270*
      5. Keeping Hasbro world headquarters in Pawtucket *270*
      6. Deferred Action for Childhood Arrivals, or DACA "Dreamers" *270*
      7. Opioid users and people with mental-health needs *271*
      8. The arts *271*
      9. Expanding solar and wind power *271*
   MY JOURNEY TO LAUNCHING MY NONPROFIT CANEIWALK 272
   SOLJANE MARTINEZ 275
   ED.D CANDIDATE, CONSULTANT, EDUCATOR, MOM 275
      My experience as an educator includes: *275*

TATIANA BAENA 277
CENTRAL FALLS CITY COUNCIL AT LARGE 277
CAMPAIGN ANNOUNCEMENT 278
OBED PAPP 280
MARIA RIVERA 280
SYLVIA BERNAL 281

Appendix 282

THE 20TH CENTURY'S LONGEST REVOLUTION STILL HAS WORK TO DO 282
RHODE ISLAND LATINO CIVIC FUND HISPANICS IN PHILANTHROPY FUNDING 286
HISPANICS IN PHILANTHROPY (HIP) 286
Grants Awarded 287
Grant Goals: 288
Grant Goals: 290
RHODE ISLAND LATINO CIVIC FUND BYLAWS 291

Rhode Island Latino Civic Fund Incorporation 304

ID Number: 000125204 304
Date of Incorporation in Rhode Island: 06-11-2002 304
Purpose: To Promote The Participation Of The Latino Community In The Civic Life And Democratic Processes Of Rhode Island Title: 7- 304

GuideStar 353

Roger Williams University deepens ties to Latino community 355

SCHOOL OF CONTINUING STUDIES PARTNERS WITH R.I. LATINO CIVIC FUND 355

RWU School of Continuing Studies Formalizes Partnership with Rhode Island Latino Civic Fund 358

PARTNERSHIP WILL PROVIDE PROGRAMS AND RESOURCES TO THE STATE'S GROWING LATINO POPULATION 358

Reference Sources 360

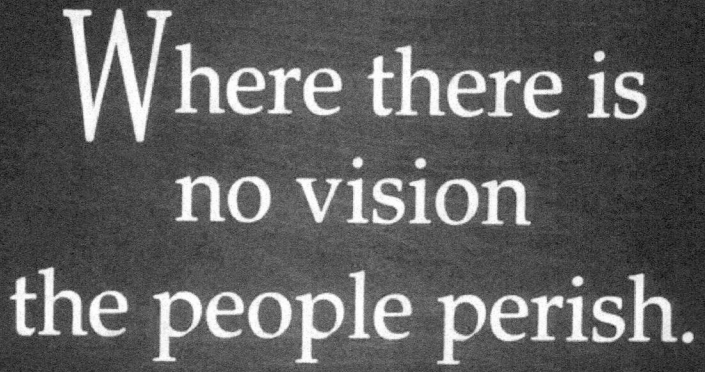

In Celebration of the 100th Anniversary of the Nineteenth Amendment to the United States Constitution and the Success of the Latina Leadership Institute

Tomás Ávila
November 30, 2019

"You can't connect the dots looking forward; you can only connect them looking backwards. So, you have to trust that the dots will somehow connect in your future." Steve Jobs

As November comes to an end, and Facebook memories reminds me that one year ago today, I made my 17 presentation to the Latina Leadership Institute (LLI) participants, one of them being Melinda Lopez who becomes the latest LLI alum to enter the political electoral fray with her Tuesday November 12, 2019 candidacy announcement for Johnston District 43 State Representative 2020 electoral cycle, I am reminded of the success of a 20 year vision developed into a plan I titled "The Latina Outreach Project" published November 1, 1999, the outgrowth of my research in preparation of RILPAC's annual fundraiser dedicated to the upcoming 80th anniversary of the passage of the 19th amendment to the U.S. Constitution, May 21, 1919 giving women the right to vote, through a resolution calling for woman suffrage passed, after much debate, at the Seneca Falls Convention in July 19th and 20th, 1848.

According to my research, the Convention was convened by Elizabeth Cady Stanton and Lucretia Mott who demanded a wide range of changes spelled out in The **Declaration of Sentiments** a document based upon the Declaration of Independence. Furthermore, according to the research after the convention, Elizabeth Cady Stanton asked, "What are we next to do?"

The women of Seneca Falls had challenged America to social revolution with a list of demands that touched every aspect of life. Testing different approaches, the early women's rights leaders came to view the ballot as the best way to change the system, but they did not limit their efforts to one issue. Fifty years after the convention, women could claim progress in property rights, employment and educational opportunities, divorce and child custody laws, and increased social freedoms. By the early 20th century, a coalition of suffragists, temperance groups, reform-minded politicians, and women's social welfare organizations mustered a successful push for the vote. Although Susan B. Anthony and Elizabeth Cady Stanton devoted 50 years to the women's suffrage movement, neither lived to see women gain the right to vote. But their work and that of many other suffragists contributed to the ultimate passage of the 19th amendment in 1920.

I also came across an excerpt of Ruth Rosen, a History Professor at UC Davis, the Author of "The World Split Open: How the Modern Women's Movement Changed America," to Be Published by Viking in February 2000, and her article; "The 20th Century's Longest Revolution Still Has Work to Do: Women now matter and society has been transformed; the next generation must assume the mantle.", stated that American women entered the 20th century without the right to vote and ended it with the right "to have it all" as long as they "do it all." Progress? It depends on whom you ask. In many ways, the women's movement has been the longest revolution of the century. American women's participation in both the labor force and the sexual revolution had dramatically altered their lives. Yet it took the modern women's movement to address the many ways women felt exploited, to lend legitimacy to their growing sense of injustice.

Perhaps the most important legacy was precisely that "women's issues" had entered mainstream national politics, where they had changed the terms of political debate. Everyday life had also changed in small but significant ways. Strangers addressed a woman as Ms.; schoolchildren learned about sexism before they became teenagers; language became more gender-neutral; popular culture saturated society with comedies, thrillers and mysteries that turned on changing gender roles. And two decades after the movement's first years, the number of women politicians doubled. Even more significant, millions of women entered jobs that once had been reserved for men. Although women had not gained the power to change institutions, they had joined men in colleges and universities in unprecedented numbers.

I also came across **Carol Hardy-Fanta's** book "Latina Politics, Latino Politics: Gender, Culture, and Political Participation in Boston" which through an in-depth study of the Latino community in Boston, addresses three key debates in American politics: how to look at the ways in which women and men envision the meaning of politics and political participation; how to understand culture and political life of expanding immigrant populations; and how to create a more participatory America. Hardy-Fanta examines critical gender differences in how politics is defined, what strategies Latina women and Latino men use to generate political participation, and how culture and gender interact in the political empowerment of the ethic communities, and challenges the notion of political apathy among Latinos and presents factors that stimulate political participation. She finds that the vision of politics promoted by Latina women? one based on connectedness, collectivity, community, and consciousness-raising? Contrasts sharply with a male political concern for status, hierarchy, and personal opportunity

Hardy-Fanta research describes a pattern of gender difference in how Latina women and Latino men in Boston perceived politics and how their different perceptions informed their ways of mobilizing the community, which Avila had also identified in Providence, Rhode Island. What also emerged was that Latinas played an active political role, a finding that challenged the invisibility of Latinas as political actors so prevalent in the political science literature. At the time there were many influential Latino men who held positions in city or state government, and influential Latina women, less for the position they held and more for the hours they spent talking to neighbors, colleagues, friends and strangers about getting involved in solving community problems. Meanwhile in Rhode Island, there were only two Latinos held positions in city or state government, Representative Anastasia Williams elected in 1992, and City Councilor Luis Aponte elected in 1998, both in Providence, but I observed the same trends as I got involved politically.

Two themes emerged from the study: **First** contrary to the Latina invisibility in mainstream political on social science literature, Latina women are political actors in Boston political community. On the contrary they were active in all areas of traditional politics including running for office, promoting voter registration, acting as links between city officials and the community and providing political education.

Even more important, they led meetings, rallied protesters, acted as community spokespersons, and mobilize Latino community residents.

Latina women made up the majority of the participants and activists in political events and have been the force behind mass mobilization efforts and political protests throughout the history of the Latino community in Boston.

Second the way Latinas talked about politics revealed a very different vision of "what is political?" Then that of Latinos, a vision that went beyond voting, elections, and office holding. In addition, how Latinas view the meaning of politics and political participation informs their mobilization strategies and makes them more effective than Latinos in mobilizing the Latino community.

As women Latinas reflected a more participatory vision of democracy than one based only on male models of politics. "This participatory vision of politics is more effective in part because it's more in tune with cultural expectations and it overcomes many of the structural constraints on Latino political participation in this country."

The above research information became the basis and seed of the "Latina Outreach Project" vision of empowering Latinas participation in Rhode Island political process I drafted November 1999, and the recruiting of my wife Eva Hulse-Avila, Margarita Guedes, Melba Depeña, Betty Bernal and Delia Smidt (Rodriguez Masjoan) to further lead the development of the project different strategies into a leadership institute modeled after the Center for Hispanic Policy & Advocacy (CHisPA) successful Community Leadership Development Initiative (CLDI), funded by the National Council of La Raza, and the Providence Civic Entrepreneur Program, funded by the Pew Charitable Foundation from which I graduated in 1997 and 1998 respectively, prior to my recruitment and successful Leadership Rhode Island (LRI), and Leadership For A Future graduation in 2000.

The Latina Outreach Project vision was committed to increasing Latina voter registration and participation in the local Political process and make significant strides to that end that evolved into the "Latina Leadership Institute" becoming a Successful Sustainable Intentional Latina Platform empowering Latinas electability across the state.

Latinas Outreach Project in the Rhode Island Political Process

Vision & Developed by:
Tomás Alberto Ávila
November 1, 1999

Introduction

The Latina Outreach Project is committed to increasing Latina voter registration and participation in the Political process and will make significant strides to that end. For the next year, the Latina Outreach Project will focus on building an infrastructure of Latina leadership and voter commitment that lead to a large Latina bloc vote for the next election cycle and years ahead.

As we enter the 2000 election cycle, it is imperative that we continue to build on the established infrastructure of Latina leadership by increasing their participation in the political process. The following focus areas, Voter Contact, Leadership Development, Fundraising, and Communication are important to continued progress.

The investment in the Latina Outreach Project and its strategies will yield significant returns in our efforts to win elections throughout this state. In preparing for the 2000 election cycle, the objectives of the Latina Outreach Project will be to build on the established infrastructure, develop strategies in those focus areas and secure resources necessary to implement the strategies.

Mission

To build an infrastructure of Latina leadership and voter commitment that leads to a large Latina voting bloc in the state of Rhode Island and targeted races.

Objectives

1. Restore and exceed the Latina vote percentage by 30% for the next election

2. Heighten the visibility of Latinas as a core constituency of the Political process
3. Ensure that the Political process's message speaks to and resonates with Latinas
4. Strengthen Latinas loyalty to the Political process
5. Institutionalize the participation of Latinas in the Political process

The Latinas Outreach Project will work to give women an equal voice in the Rhode Island political scene.

It seeks to expand the Latina political base by encouraging Latinas to run for public office and by encouraging people to participate in the political process. The Project will network with and recruit women to join them in the following actions:
1. Run for office or help women get elected;
2. Create networking opportunities for other women through local membership parties;
3. Write letters or op-ed pieces to your local newspapers and take advantage of your local access cable television programs to present a positive message about the political parties and the women in it;
4. Recruit other women to join in this effort.

Project Leadership

Margarita Guedes

Melba DePeña

Eva Hulse-Avila

Betty Bernal

Delia Rodriguez-Masjoan

Latinas Outreach Project Brainstorming

Latinas @ a Crossroad: Our Political Empowerment

Honoring the Past, Celebrating the Present & Imagining the Future

Initial Gala draft by Tomás Ávila

Keynote Speaker

Maria Echaveste, White House Public Liaison Director and Assistant to President Clinton, Congresswoman Nydia M. Velázquez, New York 12th District, Congresswoman Loreta Sanchez, California District 46

Venue

The Roger Williams Casino, Providence

Potential Sponsors

RILPAC, Commission on Women and Fleet Bank invite you to join us for the Millennium Latinas @ a Crossroad Forum & Banquet.

RI Latinas @ a Crossroad: A Celebration of Women Suffrage 80th Anniversary, Our Heritage and our Political Empowerment

Don't miss this extraordinary event, created especialmente para ti. For a whole day, Latinas @ a Crossroad will immerse you in a variety of hot topics chosen for their relevance to the modern Latina including Voters Registration, Politics.

Our distinguished panel of speakers will feature Nydia Velazquez. Ademas, para darle sabor, Latinas @ a Crossroad will treat you to breakfast, lunch, and a Banquet. Plus, network opportunity among other Latinas in the political scene.

Seating is limited, so call now to ensure your place!

The Pride of Our Century

Our list of 25 outstanding Latinas who have left their mark on the century by breaking barriers and creating opportunities for other Latinas, including Josefina "Fefa," Rosario, Patricia Martinez, Marta Martinez, Mildred Vega, Delia Smidt, Anastasia Williams, Jenny Rosario, Lydia Perez, Margarita Cepeda, Juanita Sanchez, Olga Noguera, Cynthia Garcia Coll, Tatiana Pina, Ana Maria Cano, Maria Garrido, Veinticinco mujeres extraordinarias que han dejado sus huellas en este siglo.

"Creating Your Own Destiny: Setting Goals"

Politics of Healthcare
Prospective Sponsors:
RILPAC
Johnson & Wales
Governor's Commission on Women
ProJo
Fleet Bank
Sovereign Bank
Citizens Bank
League of Women Voters

RI Latino Political Action Committee (RILPAC)

Cordially Invite You to Our 2000 Fundraiser

Women's Suffrage 80th Anniversary Celebration

Thursday, August 31
7:00 pm 9:00 pm

Sol City Gallery
891 Broad Street, Providence, RI

Congressional Resolution Designating the Month of March "Women's History Month"

Whereas American women of every race, class and ethnic background have made historic contributions to the growth and strength of our Nation in countless recorded and unrecorded ways;

Whereas American women have played and continue to play a critical economic, cultural, and social role in every sphere of the life of the Nation by constituting a significant portion of the labor force working inside and outside of the home;

Whereas American women have played a unique role throughout the history of the Nation by providing the majority of the volunteer labor force of the Nation;

Whereas American women were particularly important in the establishment of early charitable, philanthropic, and cultural institutions in our Nation;

Whereas American women of every race, class, and ethnic background served as early leaders in the forefront of every major progressive social change movement;

Whereas American women have been leaders, not only in securing their own rights of suffrage and equal opportunity, but also in the abolitionist movement, the emancipation movement, the industrial labor movement, the civil rights movement, and other movements, especially the peace movement, which create a more fair and just society for all; and

Whereas despite these contributions, the role of American women is history has been consistently overlooked and undervalued, in the literature, teaching and study of American History;

Now, therefore, be it resolved by the Senate and House of Representatives of the United States of America in Congress assembled, that March is designated as "Women's History Month." The President is authorized and requested to issue a proclamation for each of these months, calling upon the people of the United States to observe those months with appropriate programs, ceremonies and activities.

Timeline of Key Events in the American Women's Rights Movement

by Ann-Marie Imbornoni

1848	The first women's rights convention is held in Seneca Falls, New York. After 2 days of discussion and debate, 68 women and 32 men sign a Declaration of Sentiments, which outlines grievances and sets the agenda for the women's rights movement. A set of 12 resolutions is adopted calling for equal treatment of women and men under the law and voting rights for women. Top
1850	The first National Women's Rights Convention takes place in Worcester, Mass., attracting more than 1,000 participants. National conventions are held yearly (except for 1857) through 1860.
1869	**May** Susan B. Anthony and Elizabeth Cady Stanton form the National Woman Suffrage Association. The primary goal of the organization is to achieve voting rights for women by means of a Congressional amendment to the Constitution. **Nov.** Lucy Stone, Henry Blackwell, and others form the American Woman Suffrage Association. This group focuses exclusively on gaining voting rights for women through amendments to individual state constitutions. **Dec. 10** The territory of Wyoming passes the first women's suffrage law. The following year, women begin serving on juries in the territory. Top
1890	The National Women Suffrage Association and the American Women Suffrage Association merge to form the National American

Woman Suffrage Association (NAWSA). As the movement's mainstream organization, NAWSA wages state-by-state campaigns to obtain voting rights for women.

1893

Colorado is the first state to adopt an amendment granting women the right to vote. Utah and Idaho follow suit in 1896, Washington State in 1910, California in 1911, Oregon, Kansas, and Arizona in 1912, Alaska and Illinois in 1913, Montana and Nevada in 1914, New York in 1917; Michigan, South Dakota, and Oklahoma in 1918.

Top

1896

The National Association of Colored Women is formed, bringing together more than 100 black women's clubs. Leaders in the black women's club movement include Josephine St. Pierre Ruffin, Mary Church Terrell, and Anna Julia Cooper.

1903

The National Women's Trade Union League (WTUL) is established to advocate for improved wages and working conditions for women.

Top

1913

Alice Paul and Lucy Burns form the Congressional Union to work toward the passage of a federal amendment to give women the vote. The group is later renamed the National Women's Party. Members picket the White House and practice other forms of civil disobedience.

1916

Margaret Sanger opens the first U.S. birth-control clinic in Brooklyn, N.Y. Although the clinic is shut down 10 days later and Sanger is arrested, she eventually wins support through the courts and opens another clinic in New York City in 1923.

Top

1919

The federal woman suffrage amendment, originally written by Susan B. Anthony and introduced in Congress in 1878, is passed by the

		House of Representatives and the Senate. It is then sent to the states for ratification.
1920	**Aug. 26**	The Women's Bureau of the Department of Labor is formed to collect information about women in the workforce and safeguard good working conditions for women. The 19th Amendment to the Constitution, granting women the right to vote, is signed into law by Secretary of State Bainbridge Colby. Top
1921		Margaret Sanger founds the American Birth Control League, which evolves into the Planned Parenthood Federation of America in 1942.
1935		Mary McLeod Bethune organizes the National Council of Negro Women, a coalition of black women's groups that lobbies against job discrimination, racism, and sexism. Top
1936		The federal law prohibiting the dissemination of contraceptive information through the mail is modified and birth control information is no longer classified as obscene. Throughout the 1940s and 50s, birth control advocates are engaged in numerous legal suits.
1955		The Daughters of Bilitis (DOB), the first lesbian organization in the United States, is founded. Although DOB originated as a social group, it later developed into a political organization to win basic acceptance for lesbians in the United States. Top
1960		The Food and Drug Administration approves birth control pills.
1961		President John Kennedy establishes the President's Commission on the Status of Women and appoints Eleanor Roosevelt as chairwoman. The report issued by the Commission in 1963 documents substantial

	discrimination against women in the workplace and makes specific recommendations for improvement, including fair hiring practices, paid maternity leave, and affordable child care.

Top |
| **1963** | Betty Friedan publishes her highly influential book *The Feminine Mystique*, which describes the dissatisfaction felt by middle-class American housewives with the narrow role imposed on them by society. The book becomes a best-seller and galvanizes the modern women's rights movement.

June 10
Congress passes the Equal Pay Act, making it illegal for employers to pay a woman less than what a man would receive for the same job.

Top |
| **1964** | Title VII of the Civil Rights Act bars discrimination in employment on the basis of race and sex. At the same time it establishes the Equal Employment Opportunity Commission (EEOC) to investigate complaints and impose penalties. |
| **1965** | In *Griswold v. Connecticut*, the Supreme Court strikes down the one remaining state law prohibiting the use of contraceptives by married couples.

Top |
| **1966** | The National Organization for Women (NOW) is founded by a group of feminists including Betty Friedan. The largest women's rights group in the U.S., NOW seeks to end sexual discrimination, especially in the workplace, by means of legislative lobbying, litigation, and public demonstrations. |
| **1967** | Executive Order 11375 expands President Lyndon Johnson's affirmative action policy of 1965 to cover discrimination based on gender. As a result, federal agencies and contractors must take active |

measures to ensure that women as well as minorities enjoy the same educational and employment opportunities as white males.

Top

1968

The EEOC rules that sex-segregated help wanted ads in newspapers are illegal. This ruling is upheld in 1973 by the Supreme Court, opening the way for women to apply for higher-paying jobs hitherto open only to men.

1969

California becomes the first state to adopt a "no fault" divorce law, which allows couples to divorce by mutual consent. By 1985 every state has adopted a similar law. Laws are also passed regarding the equal division of common property.

Top

1970

In *Schultz* v. *Wheaton Glass Co.*, a U.S. Court of Appeals rules that jobs held by men and women need to be "substantially equal" but not "identical" to fall under the protection of the Equal Pay Act. An employer cannot, for example, change the job titles of women workers in order to pay them less than men.

Top

1971

Ms. Magazine is first published as a sample insert in *New York* magazine; 300,000 copies are sold out in 8 days. The first regular issue is published in July 1972. The magazine becomes the major forum for feminist voices, and cofounder and editor Gloria Steinem is launched as an icon of the modern feminist movement.

Mar. 22

1972

The Equal Rights Amendment (ERA) is passed by Congress and sent to the states for ratification. Originally drafted by Alice Paul in 1923, the amendment reads: "Equality of rights under the law shall not be denied or abridged by the United States or by any State on account of sex." The amendment died in 1982 when it failed to achieve ratification by a minimum of 38 states.

Also on Mar. 22
In *Eisenstadt v. Baird* the Supreme Court rules that the right to privacy includes an unmarried person's right to use contraceptives.

June 23
Title IX of the Education Amendments bans sex discrimination in schools. It states: "No person in the United States shall, on the basis of sex, be excluded from participation in, be denied the benefits of, or be subjected to discrimination under any educational program or activity receiving federal financial assistance." As a result of Title IX, the enrollment of women in athletics programs and professional schools increases dramatically.

Top

1973

As a result of [Roe v. Wade,](#) the Supreme Court establishes a woman's right to safe and legal abortion, overriding the anti-abortion laws of many states.

1974

The Equal Credit Opportunity Act prohibits discrimination in consumer credit practices on the basis of sex, race, marital status, religion, national origin, age, or receipt of public assistance.

In *Corning Glass Works* v. *Brennan*, the U.S. Supreme Court rules that employers cannot justify paying women lower wages because that is what they traditionally received under the "going market rate." A wage differential occurring "simply because men would not work at the low rates paid women" is unacceptable.

Top

1976

The first marital rape law is enacted in [Nebraska,](#) making it illegal for a husband to rape his wife.

1978

The Pregnancy Discrimination Act bans employment discrimination against pregnant women. Under the Act, a woman cannot be fired or denied a job or a promotion because she is or may become pregnant,

25

	nor can she be forced to take a pregnancy leave if she is willing and able to work. Top
1984	EMILY's List (Early Money Is Like Yeast) is established as a financial network for pro-choice Democratic women running for national political office. The organization makes a significant impact on the increasing numbers of women elected to Congress.
1986	*Meritor Savings Bank v. Vinson*, the Supreme Court finds that sexual harassment is a form of illegal job discrimination. Top
1992	In *Planned Parenthood v. Casey*, the Supreme Court reaffirmed the validity of a woman's right to abortion under *Roe v. Wade*. The case successfully challenged Pennsylvania's 1989 Abortion Control Act, which sought to reinstate restrictions previously ruled unconstitutional.
1994	The Violence Against Women Act tightens federal penalties for sex offenders, funds services for victims of rape and domestic violence, and provides for special training of police officers.

The Declaration of Sentiments
Seneca Falls, New York, 1848

Source: U.S. Dept. of State

The Declaration of Sentiments and Resolutions was drafted by Elizabeth Cady Stanton for the women's rights convention at Seneca Falls, New York in 1848. Based on the American Declaration of Independence, the Sentiments demanded equality with men before the law, in education and employment. Here, too, was the first pronouncement demanding that women be given the right to vote.

Sentiments

When, in the course of human events, it becomes necessary for one portion of the family of man to assume among the people of the earth a position different from that which they have hitherto occupied, but one to which the laws of nature and of nature's God entitle them, a decent respect to the opinions of mankind requires that they should declare the causes that impel them to such a course.

We hold these truths to be self-evident: that all men and women are created equal; that they are endowed by their Creator with certain inalienable rights; that among these are life, liberty, and the pursuit of happiness; that to secure these rights governments are instituted, deriving their just powers from the consent of the governed. Whenever any form of government becomes destructive of these ends, it is the right of those who suffer from it to refuse allegiance to it, and to insist upon the institution of a new government, laying its foundation on such principles, and organizing its powers in such form, as to them shall seem most likely to effect their safety and happiness.

Prudence, indeed, will dictate that governments long established should not be changed for light and transient causes; and, accordingly, all experience has shown that mankind are more disposed to suffer, while evils are sufferable, than to right themselves by abolishing the forms to which they were accustomed. But when a long train of abuses and usurpations, pursuing invariably the same object, evinces a design to reduce them under absolute despotism, it is their duty to throw off such government and to provide new guards for their future security. Such has been the patient sufferance of the women under this government, and such is now the necessity which constrains them to demand the equal station to which they are entitled.

The history of mankind is a history of repeated injuries and usurpations on the part of man toward woman, having in direct object the establishment of an absolute tyranny over her. To prove this, let facts be submitted to a candid world.

He has never permitted her to exercise her inalienable right to the elective franchise.
He has compelled her to submit to law in the formation of which she had no voice.

He has withheld from her rights which are given to the most ignorant and degraded men, both natives and foreigners.

Having deprived her of this first right as a citizen, the elective franchise, thereby leaving her without representation in the halls of legislation, he has oppressed her on all sides.

He has made her, if married, in the eye of the law, civilly dead. He has taken from her all right in property, even to the wages she earns.
He has made her morally, an irresponsible being, as she can commit many crimes with impunity, provided they be done in the presence of her husband. In the covenant of marriage, she is compelled to promise obedience to her husband, he becoming, to all intents and purposes, her master-the law giving him power to deprive her of her liberty and to administer chastisement.

He has so framed the laws of divorce, as to what shall be the proper causes and, in case of separation, to whom the guardianship of the children shall be given, as to be wholly regardless of the happiness of the women-the law, in all cases, going upon a false supposition of the supremacy of man and giving all power into his hands.

After depriving her of all rights as a married woman, if single and the owner of property, he has taxed her to support a government which recognizes her only when her property can be made profitable to it.

He has monopolized nearly all the profitable employments, and from those she is permitted to follow, she receives but a scanty remuneration. He closes against her all the avenues to wealth and distinction which he considers most honorable to himself. As a teacher of theology, medicine, or law, she is not known.

He has denied her the facilities for obtaining a thorough education, all colleges being closed against her.

He allows her in church, as well as state, but a subordinate position, claiming apostolic authority for her exclusion from the ministry, and, with some exceptions, from any public participation in the affairs of the church.

He has created a false public sentiment by giving to the world a different code of morals for men and women, by which moral delinquencies which exclude women from society are not only tolerated but deemed of little account in man.

He has usurped the prerogative of Jehovah himself, claiming it as his right to assign for her a sphere of action, when that belongs to her conscience and to her God.

He has endeavored, in every way that he could, to destroy her confidence in her own powers, to lessen her self-respect, and to make her willing to lead a dependent and abject life.

Now, in view of this entire disfranchisement of one-half the people of this country, their social and religious degradation, in view of the unjust laws above mentioned, and because women do feel themselves aggrieved, oppressed, and fraudulently deprived of their most sacred rights, we insist that they have immediate admission to all the rights and privileges which belong to them as citizens of the United States.

In entering upon the great work before us, we anticipate no small amount of misconception, misrepresentation, and ridicule; but we shall use every instrumentality within our power to effect our object. We shall employ agents, circulate tracts, petition the state and national legislatures, and endeavor to enlist the pulpit and the press in our behalf. We hope this Convention will be followed by a series of conventions embracing every part of the country.

Resolutions

Whereas, the great precept of nature is conceded to be that "man shall pursue his own true and substantial happiness." Blackstone in his Commentaries remarks that this law of nature, being coeval with mankind and dictated by God himself, is, of course, superior in obligation to any other. It is binding over all the globe, in all countries and at all times; no human laws are of any validity if contrary to this, and such of them as are valid derive all their force, and all their validity, and all their authority, mediately and immediately, from this original; therefore,

Resolved, That such laws as conflict, in any way, with the true and substantial happiness of woman, are contrary to the great precept of nature and of no validity, for this is superior in obligation to any other.

Resolved, that all laws which prevent woman from occupying such a station in society as her conscience shall dictate, or which place her in a position inferior to that of man, are contrary to the great precept of nature and therefore of no force or authority.

Resolved, that woman is man's equal, was intended to be so by the Creator, and the highest good of the race demands that she should be recognized as such.

Resolved, that the women of this country ought to be enlightened in regard to the laws under which they live, that they may no longer publish their degradation by declaring themselves satisfied with their present position, nor their ignorance, by asserting that they have all the rights they want.

Resolved, that inasmuch as man, while claiming for himself intellectual superiority, does accord to woman moral superiority, it is preeminently his duty to encourage her to speak and teach, as she has an opportunity, in all religious assemblies.

Resolved, that the same amount of virtue, delicacy, and refinement of behavior that is required of woman in the social state also be required of man, and the same transgressions should be visited with equal severity on both man and woman.

Resolved, that the objection of indelicacy and impropriety, which is so often brought against woman when she addresses a public audience, comes with a very ill grace from those who encourage, by their attendance, her appearance on the stage, in the concert, or in feats of the circus.

Resolved, that woman has too long rested satisfied in the circumscribed limits which corrupt customs and a perverted application of the Scriptures have marked out for her, and that it is time she should move in the enlarged sphere which her great Creator has assigned her.

Resolved, that it is the duty of the women of this country to secure to themselves their sacred right to the elective franchise.

Resolved, that the equality of human rights results necessarily from the fact of the identity of the race in capabilities and responsibilities.

Resolved, that the speedy success of our cause depends upon the zealous and untiring efforts of both men and women for the overthrow of the monopoly of the pulpit, and for the securing to woman an equal participation with men in the various trades, professions, and commerce.

Resolved, therefore, that, being invested by the Creator with the same capabilities and same consciousness of responsibility for their exercise, it is demonstrably the right and duty of woman, equally with man, to promote every righteous cause by every righteous means; and especially in regard to the great subjects of morals and religion, it is self-evidently her right to participate with her brother in teaching them, both in private and in public, by writing and by speaking, by any instrumentalities proper to be used, and in any assemblies proper to be held; and this being a self-evident truth growing out of the divinely implanted principles of human nature, any custom or authority adverse to it, whether modern or wearing the hoary sanction of antiquity, is to be regarded as a self-evident falsehood, and at war with mankind.

Amendment XIX

(The proposed amendment was sent to the states June 4, 1919, by the Sixty-sixth Congress. It was ratified Aug. 18, 1920.)

[The right of citizens to vote shall not be denied because of sex.]

The right of citizens of the United States to vote shall not be denied or abridged by the United States or by any State on account of sex.

[Congress given power to enforce this article.]
Congress shall have power to enforce this article by appropriate legislation.

Destino 2002: Latina Political Empowerment Project

Created by Melba Depeña and Tomás Ávila

The Need

According to the U. S. Census, Latinos are expected to be the largest ethnic group in the United States by the year 2010. However, current statistics indicate that while 30 million Latinos are eligible voters, only five percent exercises this power. As a result of this lack of participation in the political process, Latinos continue to be underrepresented at the local, state and national level of the US government. Potentially, the Latino vote can have a great impact, yet, as a community Latinos have not recognized and value this power. This concern is particularly intricate for Latinas (women of Hispanic descent). Traditionally, Latinas have not been active participants in politics because it has been viewed as an area reserved for men.

Over the last few decades, women have made great progress by assuming positions of social prominence to contribute to the improvement of the American society. For example, more women are enrolling and graduating from institutions of higher learning than ever before, the number of women owned and led business is increasing, and the success in the political arena has been remarkable. Women have assumed political leadership roles at the local, state and national levels of government, (**list examples**). As they embark upon this challenging journey towards increase political power they are faced with some of the traditional obstacles. The fact that some women have broken through the glass ceiling is an indication of sporadic and non-systematic heroic efforts.

While women continuing to search for these types of opportunities, there is still a segment that is ignored. This group of women is Latinas. While Latinas are making waves in education and the workplace, they are lacking in business ownership and notably in the area of politics. Latinas have primarily concentrated on grassroots and community efforts. In the state of Rhode Island, we have been fortunate to have prominent community activists such as Juanita Sanchez, who before her passing fought for the rights of immigrants and Margarita Cepeda who mentored so many of our youth. However, none of these prominent community activists have ascended to political office, this is the missing link in order to establish full participation and representation of the historically underrepresented Latinas.

The Goal

For the next two years, the Latina Political Project will focus on building an infrastructure of Latina leadership and voter commitment that will lead to a larger Latina bloc vote for the 2002 election cycle and years ahead. The Latina Political Project is committed to increase the participation of Latinas in the State of Rhode Island. This goal will be accomplished through training, voter registration, and Get Out The Vote (GOTV) efforts. The long-term goal of this project is to encourage Latinas to run for local and state office. This project will serve as a pilot or model program that hopefully in the future will be expanded to include other underrepresented

RHODE ISLAND

Destino 2002: Latina Political Empowerment Project

Created by Melba Depena and Tomas Avila
groups of women such as African American, Asian and Anglos. The targeting of the smaller group of women is to ensure greater possibility of success, tracking and measuring results.

The Objectives

The Latina Political Project has been designed as a two-year, non-partisan initiative that will address the following objectives:
- To encourage greater involved in the political process

- To identify and train Latinas who are interested in running for office
- To increase Latinas awareness of the political process
- Increase Latina's participation in key areas such as education, business and community
- Identify and address issues that hinder Latinas participation in politics
- Develop and implement a venue to register Latinas to vote through collaboration of
- national and local organizations
- Track and quantify results

The Program

The Latina Political Project will consist of three components, which will effectively address and implement the goal and objectives.
See enclosed tentative agenda)

1) Latinas At a Cross Road Conference
   1. August 26, 2000 will mark the 80th anniversary of the 19th amendment to the U.S. Constitution, which granted women the right to vote.

2) Political Training Institute
   The overall goal of this program is to encourage more civic participation among women, that in turn will foster an enhanced awareness of community involvement. The institute will offer the opportunity to further develop core leadership skills that are readily transferable to keys areas such as education, health and political empowerment. This goal will be accomplished through a series of monthly workshops addressing the following issues:
   a. Writing Skills
   b. Public Speaking Skills
   c. Fundraising Skills
   d. Personal Assessment

3) Civic Awareness Campaign
   e. Voter Registration
   f. Outreach and education

  g. Get Out The Vote (GOTV)

Destino 2002: Latina Political Empowerment Project
Created by Melba Depena and Tomas Avila

Conference: Latinas at A Cross Road

8:30am-9:30am Registration and Network
9:30am-10:30am Adelante Hacia Nuestro Destino Breakfast
Welcome by Rep. Anastasia Williams

10:45am-12:00pm Plenary: The importance of Latinas Participation in the political process

12:15pm-1:15pm Lunch
1:30pm-2:30pm Symposium: Preparing Ourselves For The Challenge
2:30pm-3:00pm Closing Remarks For the Conference
6:00pm-12:00pm Celebrating Latina Leadership Dinner
Convention Center or RI Foundation

- Award: Latina local political leader will be honored
- Keynote Speaker: Latina national political leader

Proposed Calendar of Events For Latina Political Institute

August 26, 2000

- Kick-off/Press Conference In conjunction with other community organizations (ChisPA, Progreso Latino, Quisqueya In Action, RILPAC, Commission on Women etc)

September 2000

Latinas in Politics: A Secret Well Kept. A comprehensive political training session (topics will include technology, voter contact, public speaking, fundraising, public relations, campaign plan)
- Develop strategy of identifying potential Latina candidates to run for elected office.

- Building coalitions (with men, other women, i.e. African American, White, Asian)
- Identifying the difference between grassroots and electoral efforts

October 2000

Politics 101: Public Speaking
I am making my point: How to become an effective communicator

November 2000

- Politics 101: Political Writing

December 2000

- Roundtable Discussion This event will rally women, professional, civic, and community organizations. Through face to face meetings with the State's top policy makers, the participants will maximize their influence.

- With local political Latina leaders

January 2001

- Politics 101: Fundraising
- (Ocean State Action, NALEO, Common Cause, Governors Commission on Women, RI League
- of Women Voters)

Destino 2002: Latina Political Empowerment Project
Created by Melba Depeña and Tomás Ávila

The Need

According to the Census, Latinos are expected to be the largest ethnic group in the United States by the year 2010. However, current statistics indicates that while 30 million Latinos are eligible voters, only five percent exercises this power. As a result of this lack of participation in the political process, Latinos continue to be underrepresented at the local, state and national level of the US government. Potentially, the Latino vote can have a great impact, yet, as a community Latinos have not recognized and value this power. This concern is particularly intricate for Latinas (women of Hispanic descent). Traditionally, Latinos have not been active participants in politics because it has been viewed as an area reserved for men.

Over the last few decades, women have made great progress by assuming positions of social prominence to contribute to the improvement of the American society. For example, more women are enrolling and graduating from institutions of higher learning then ever before, the number of women owned and led business is increasing, and the success in the political arena has been remarkable. Women have assumed political leadership roles at the local, state and national levels of government, (list examples). As they embark upon this challenging journey towards increase political power they are faced with some of the traditional obstacles. The fact that some women have broken through the glass ceiling is an indication of speratic and non-systematic heroic efforts.

While women continuing to search for these types of opportunities, there is still a segment that is ignored. This group of women is Latinas. While Latinas are making waves in education and the work place, they are lacking in business ownership and notably in the area politics. Latinas have primarily concentrated on grassroots and community efforts. In the state of Rhode Island, we have been fortunate to have prominent community activists such as Juanita Sanchez, who before her passing fought for the rights of immigrants and Margarita Cepeda who mentored so many of our youth. However, none of these prominent community activists have ascended to political office, this is the missing link in order to establish full participation and representation of the historically underrepresented Latinas.

The Goal

For the next two years, the Latina Political Project will focus on building an infrastructure of Latina leadership and voter commitment that will lead to a larger Latina bloc vote for the 2002 election cycle and years ahead. The Latina Political Project is committed to increase the participation of Latinas in the State of Rhode Island. This goal will be accomplished through training, voter registration, and Get Out The Vote (GOTV)

Destino 2002: Latina Political Empowerment Project
Created by Melba Depena and Tomas Avila

efforts. The long-term goal of this project is to encourage Latinas to run for local and state office. This project will serve as a pilot or model program that hopefully in the future will be expanded to include other underrepresented groups of women such as African American, Asian and Anglos. The targeting of the smaller group of women is to ensure greater possibility of success, tracking and measuring results.

The Objectives

The Latina Political Project has been designed as a two-year, non-partisan initiative that will address the following objectives:

- To encourage greater involved in the political process
- To identify and train Latinas who are interested in running for office
- To increase Latinas awareness of the political process
- Increase Latina

Destino 2002: Latina Political Empowerment Project
Created by Melba Depena and Tomas Avila

- Voter Registration
- Outreach and education
- Get Out The Vote (GOTV)

Conference:

Latinas At A Cross Road

8:30am-9:30am	**Registration and Network**
9:30am-10:30am	**Adelante Hacia Nuestro Destino Breakfast** Welcome by Rep. Anastasia Williams
10:45am-12:00pm	**Plenary: The importance of Latinas Participation in the political process**
12:15pm-1:15pm	**Lunch**
1:30pm-2:30pm	**Symposium: Preparing Ourselves For The Challenge**
2:30pm-3:00pm	**Closing Remarks For the Conference**
6:00pm-12:00pm	**Celebrating Latina Leadership Dinner** **Convention Center or RI Foundation**

- Award: Latina local political leader will be honored
- Keynote Speaker: Latina national political leader

Destino 2002: Latina Political Empowerment Project
Created by Melba Depena and Tomas Avila

Proposed Calendar of Events For
Latina Political Institute

August 26, 2000
Kick-off/Press Conference
In conjunction with other community organizations (ChisPA, Progreso Latino, Quisqueya In Action, RILPAC, Commission on Women etc)

September 2000
Latinas in Politics: A Secret Well Kept. A comprehensive political training session (topics will include technology, voter contact, public speaking, fundraising, public relations, campaign plan)

- Develop strategy of identifying potential Latina candidates to run for elected office.

- Building coalitions (with men, other women, i.e. African American, White, Asian)

- Identifying the difference between grassroots and electoral efforts

October 2000
Politics 101: Public Speaking
I am making my point: How to become an effective communicator

November 2000
Politics 101: Political Writing

December 2000
Roundtable Discussion This event will rally women, professional, civic, and community organizations. Through face to face meetings with the State's top policy makers, the participants will maximize their influence.

With local political Latina leaders

January 2001
Politics 101: Fundraising

(Ocean State Action, NALEO, Common Cause, Governors Commission on Women, RI League of Women Voters)

Destino 2002: Latina Political Empowerment Project
Created by Melba Depena and Tomas Avila

Key Organizations

- Commission On Women
- Rhode Island League of Women Voters
- Rhode Island Latino Political Action Committee
- Providence Journal
- Fleet National Bank
- Sovereign Bank
- Rhode Island Foundation

Destino 2002: Latina Political Empowerment Project
Created by Melba Depena and Tomas Avila

HISPANAS ORGANIZED FOR POLITICAL EQUALITY
"Inspiring Latina Leadership"

MISSION STATEMENT

HOPE, founded in 1989, is a non-profit, non-partisan, advocacy organization dedicated to the political education and participation of Latinas and other women in the political process. HOPE has anchored itself to the principle that knowledge of the political process coupled with active participation will fuel powerful and necessary change with benefits transcending the Latina community to the community at large.

PROGRAMS

HOPE Leadership Institute - "Strengthening Latina Leadership"

The *HOPE Leadership Institute (HLI)* was established to fill an unmet need to provide leadership,

civic and skills training to California

Destino 2002: Latina Political Empowerment Project
Created by Melba Depena and Tomas Avila

Voter Empowerment Workshop Series

The series highlights current public policy that directly impacts the Latino community in hopes of empowering the Latina citizenry in the voting booth. This series has included discussions with key policy makers such as U.S. Senate Majority Leader George Mitchell, Willie Brown, Lieutenant Governor Gray Davis, Federal Communications Commissioner Reed Hundt, State Controller Kathy Connell, Speaker Cruz Bustamante, Secretary of Energy Bill Richardson and Secretary of the U.S. Army Louis Caldera.

Destino 2002: Latina Political Empowerment Project
Created by Melba Depena and Tomas Avila

2002 The Rhode Island Latino Civic Fund (RILCF) Established

The Rhode Island Latino Civic Fund (RILCF) was established in 2002 with the purpose of promoting the civic education, registration, and participation of Latinos in the state of Rhode Island. In addition, the organization is actively involved in educating and informing elected officials about the issues and concerns impacting the Latino community in Rhode Island.

RILCF has remained united by its shared commitment to equality and justice. The organization strives to create a community where every Rhode Islanders has access to quality education, healthcare, housing, and livable wage jobs that support them and their respective families achieve their full potential. Furthermore, RILCF aims to accomplish its goals and overarching purpose by doing the following:

1. Promoting the participation of the Latino community in the civic life and democratic processes of Rhode Island through activities, such as those that increase voter education, voter registration and voter anticipation.

2. Raising awareness in the Latino community regarding public policy issues benefiting Latinos and other individuals from urban communities as well as those that could adversely impact the Latino community.

3. Ensuring that elected officials, political leaders and candidates have a broad understanding of the concerns and priorities among Rhode Island Latinos.

2003 Rhode Island Foundation Latina Leadership Institute Letter of Intent

Melba Depena & Delia Rodriguez Masjoan

February 26, 2003

Simone P. Joyaux
The Women's Fund of Rhode Island
One Union Station
Providence, RI 02903

Dear Ms. Joyaux:

The Latina Leadership Institute is delighted to submit this Letter of Intent to be considered for the Women's Fund Grant. We are excited about coordinating the first Annual Latina Political Symposium 2005 and hope that you can give us the opportunity to submit a full proposal.

Organization Mission Statement:
The Latina Leadership Institute is committed to promoting the participation of Latinas in leadership positions through hands-on training, professional and leadership development, political participation and voluntarism.

Project Description:
The Latina Political Symposium is an idea that emerged during our first-year evaluation of the Latina Leadership Institute. During the Institute the participants expressed an interest in further evaluating Latina Political participation. The project will include 3 modules:

- Voter Registration and Voter Education: This is developed to encourage Latinas to register to vote while promoting the need to learn about the political process of the state.

- Political Training: This is designed to assist any women who may be interested in running for office or coordinating a campaign.

❏ Political Activism: This is designed to motivate Latinas to continue involved in the political system by becoming volunteers.

Latinas have been the backbone of the Latino community's increasing civic participation within our state. These women serve as volunteers in campaigns, as coordinators at health fairs and many more community activities. Consequently, there is a dire need to formally provide guidance and information so they can utilize these new skills to better serve the community at different levels of our community.

Latinas need the tools to further develop knowledge, skills and abilities that will place them into leadership positions, and actively participate in all sector of the community. We are excited about all the wonderful opportunities that lie ahead for our community, and trust that this first Annual Latina Political Symposium will contribute to the overall improvement of our state.

The Women's fund of Rhode Island has a strong commitment to providing women equal access to opportunities in social, economic, education and political aspects. We are certain that the Annual Latina Political Symposium will serve as catalyst through which this can be accomplished.

Please feel free to contact us. Thank you for considering our request.

Sincerely,

Melba Depena   Delia Rodriguez Masjoan
721-9900   462-0524

2003 Latina Leadership Institute

The Latina Leadership Institute is delighted to submit this Letter of Intent to be considered for the Women's Fund Grant. We are excited about coordinating the first Annual Latina Political Symposium 2005 and hope that you can give us the opportunity to submit a full proposal.

Organization Mission Statement

The Latina Leadership Institute is committed to promoting the participation of Latinas in leadership positions through hands-on training, professional and leadership development, political participation and voluntarism.

Project Description

The Latina Political Symposium is an idea that emerged during our first-year evaluation of the Latina Leadership Institute. During the Institute the participants expressed an interest in further evaluating Latina Political participation. The project will include 3 modules:
- Voter Registration and Voter Education: This is developed to encourage Latinas to register to vote while promoting the need to learn about the political process of the state.
- Political Training: This is designed to assist any women who may be interested in running for office or coordinating a campaign.
- Political Activism: This is designed to motivate Latinas to continue involved in the political system by becoming volunteers.

Latinas have been the backbone of the Latino community's increasing civic participation within our state. These women serve as volunteers in campaigns, as coordinators at health fairs and many more community activities. Consequently, there is a dire need to formally provide guidance and information so they can utilize these new skills to better serve the community at different levels of our community.

Latinas need the tools to further develop knowledge, skills and abilities that will place them into leadership positions, and actively participate in all sector of the community. We are excited about all the wonderful opportunities that lie ahead for our community, and trust that this first

Annual Latina Political Symposium will contribute to the overall improvement of our state.

The Women's fund of Rhode Island has a strong commitment to providing women equal access to opportunities in social, economic, education and political aspects. We are certain that the Annual Latina Political Symposium will serve as catalyst through which this can be accomplished.

The Need

According to the Census, Latinos are the largest ethnic group in the United States. However, current statistics indicates that Latinos in Rhode Island continue to struggle as they organize socially and politically. An important segment of this community are Latino women who have been working diligently for social change. Over the last few decades, women have made great progress by assuming positions of social prominence to contribute to the improvement of our state. While Latinas are making waves in education and the workplace, they are lacking in business ownership and notably in the area of political involvement. Latinas have primarily concentrated on grassroots and community efforts. As Latinas embark upon this challenging journey towards increasing community organizing and political participation the need for formal training is more prevalent.

The Goal

The Latina Leadership Institute is committed to increase the participation of Latinas in leadership positions and political involvement. This goal will be accomplished the ugh training in voter registration, community organizing and political participation. This project will serve as a pilot or model program that in the future will be expanded to include more in depth research. We have decided to target a small group of women to ensure greater possibility of success, tracking and measuring results.

The Objectives

The Latina Leadership Institute has been designed as initiative that will address the following objectives:

- To encourage greater involvement in civic participation To increase Latinas awareness of the political process To increase Latina's participation in key areas such as education, business and community.

- To identify and address issues that hinder Latina's participation

- To develop and implement a venue to register Latinas to vote through collaboration of national and local organizations

Press Release

The RI Latino Civic Fund announces the Graduation of the First Latina Leadership Institute Class. The graduation will take place on Tuesday August 26th, 2003 at 6:00 p. m. at the Roger Williams Casino in Providence, RI. This celebration coincides with the Anniversary of the Women's Suffrage Movement.

Thirty Latinas were selected to participate in this seven week training were they learned skills geared to providing hands-on training about community organizing, leadership skills, political involvement and advocacy to name a few. The program consisted of seven sections every two weeks for 3 1/2 hours each section. We selected 30 participants out of 92 Latinas who applied for the training, with the goal of completing the program by August, to celebrate the Suffrage Movement.

"This is a great opportunity for Latinas to learn about the community and become actively involved in the development of the community at large." Said Melba Depeña, President of the RI Latino Civic Fund.

The institute is funded by the Rhode Island Foundation with additional support from Mayor Cicilline and Secretary of State Mathew Brown.

The role of Latinas in mobilization and community organizing is one area where research has presented consistent findings. Latinas have always been involved in this type of political activity, have very often had significant leadership roles, and have also made explicit linkages between the workplace and formal arenas of politics.

This literature does not explicitly compare Latinas to Latino men. Reported findings, however, demonstrate that it is one area where Latinas have had clear and consistent success. We subdivide our discussion of the role of Latinas in political mobilization and community organizing into three distinct components: historical presence, consistent leadership, work and political connectedness, and participation in explicitly political organizations.

First Name	Last Name	Address	City	State	Zip	Email	Phone		
Maria	Acevedo	6 Norwich Ave. 2nd Floor	Providence	RI	02905		941-6940		
Dansi	Acevedo-Aleman	285 Huxley Ave.	Providence	RI	02908	alemanqo@aol.com	751-5657		
Ines	Aldas	177 Belleview Ave.	Providence	RI	02907		270-9782		
Tomasina	Almonte	18 Ryder Ave.	Cranston	RI	02920	461-8080	323-1493	461-8080	
Carolina	Bolanos		Providence	RI					
Maritza	Cabrera	232 Bay View Ave.	Cranston	RI	02883		941-3254		
Mercedes	Cabrera	11 Woodman St.	Providence	RI	02907				
Lilian	Campos	51 Thackary St. Apt. # 1	Providence	RI	02907		781-9984		
Beatriz	Caro	61 Tapan St.	Providence	RI	02908	bcaroquio@yahoo.com	521-6373		
Amanda	Carrasco	12 Iris Drive	Cranston	RI	02920		946-3264		
Marizol	De Jesus	59 Hamilton St.	Providence	RI	02907		861-4607		
Elizabeth	Eguez	346 Union St.	Providence	RI	02909		943-4207		
Rosalba	Estrada	10 Madison Ave.	Central Falls	RI	02863		728-9837		
Mercedes	Fernandez	95 Home St.	Providence	RI	02908		421-3342		
Rosalba	Garcia	133 Ontario St.	Providence	RI	02907		241-9586		
Yvonne	Grullon	91 Stanton St.	Providence	RI	02909		943-2748		
Maria	Gurierrez	41 Harvest St.	Providence	RI	02908	mama17429@latinmail.con	273-3340		
Aridia	Jennings	115 Sinclair Ave.	Providence	RI	02907		580-4297		
Eva	Jimenez	57 Putnam St.	Providence	RI	02909		751-7741		
Carmen	Lorenzo	142 Moorefield St.	Providence	RI	02909		943-8332		
Sabina	Matos	35 Florence St.	Providence	RI	02909	msabina@msn.com	383-3814		
Doris	Mejia	28 Willow St. Apt. 2	Providence	RI	02909		861-1978		
Caren	Mendez	93 Painc Ave.	Cransron	RI	02910	carenmendez@aol.com	258-8519		
Yocasta	Mendez	72 East St.	West Warwick	RI	02893	yoeastamendez@aol.com	822-0093		
Carmen	Mirabal	35 Rand St.	Central Falls	RI	02863		725-1365		
Edna	Mojica	81 West Cliftford st.	Providence	RI	02907		499-2233		
Lesbia	Pabon	13 Moorefield St.	Providence	RI	02909		943-9571		
Johanna	Petrarca	50 Monument St	Cranston	RI	02910		726-8413		
Dolores	Rodriguez	9 Hall St.	Providence	RI	02904		270-6523		
Natalia	Rosa-Sosa	175 Tide Water Dr.	Warwick	RI	02889		451-9646		

2003 LLI Graduates

First Name	Last Name
Maria	Acevedo
Dansi	Acevedo-Aleman
Ines	Aldas
Tomasina	Almonte
Carolina	Bolanos
Maritza	Cabrera
Mercedes	Cabrera
Lilian	Campos
Beatriz	Caro
Amanda	Carrasco
Marizol	De Jesus
Elizabeth	Eguez
Rosalba	Estrada
Mercedes	Fernandez
Rosalba	Garcia
Yvonne	Grullon
Maria	Gurierrez
Aridia	Jennings
Eva	Jimenez **(RIP)**
Carmen	Lorenzo
Sabina	Matos
Doris	Mejia
Caren	Mendez
Yocasta	Mendez
Carmen	Mirabal
Edna	Mojica
Lesbia	Pabon
Johanna	Petrarca
Dolores	Rodriguez
Natalia	Rosa-Sosa

Contact: Melba Depeña

Phone: (401) 277-5202

Informational bulletin

30 Latinas Graduate from the Latina Leadership Institute

Providence, RI ~ The RI Latino Civic Fund announces the Graduation of the First Latina Leadership Institute Class. The graduation will take place on Tuesday August 26th, 2003 at 6:00 p. m. at the Roger Williams Casino in Providence, RI. This celebration coincides with the Anniversary of the Women's Suffrage Movement.

Thirty Latinas were selected to participate in this seven-week training were they learned skills geared to providing hands-on training about community organizing, leadership skills, political involvement and advocacy to name a few. The program consisted of seven sections every two weeks for 3 1/2 hours each section. We selected 30 participants out of 92 Latinas who applied for the training, with the goal of completing the program by August, to celebrate the Suffrage Movement.

"This is a great opportunity for Latinas to learn about the community and become actively involved in the development of the community at large." Said Melba Depeña, President of the RI Latino Civic Fund.

The institute is funded by the Rhode Island Foundation with additional support from Mayor Cicilline and Secretary of State Mathew Brown.

Contact: Melba Depeña
Phone: (401) 277-5202

Informational bulletin
....

30 Latinas Graduate from the Latina Leadership Institute

Providence, RI ~ The RI Latino Civic Fund announces the Graduation of the First Latina Leadership Institute Class. The graduation will take place on Tuesday August 26th, 2003 at 6:00 p.m. at the Roger Williams Casino in Providence, RI. This celebration coincides with the Anniversary of the Women's Suffrage Movement.

Thirty Latinas were selected to participate in this seven week training were they learned skills geared to providing hands-on training about community organizing, leadership skills, political involvement and advocacy to name a few. The program consisted of seven sections every two weeks for 3 1/2 hours each section. We selected 30 participants out of 92 Latinas who applied for the training, with the goal of completing the program by August, to celebrate the Suffrage Movement.

"This is a great opportunity for Latinas to learn about the community and become actively involved in the development of the community at large." Said Melba Depeña, President of the RI Latino Civic Fund.

The institute is funded by the Rhode Island Foundation with additional support from Mayor Cicilline and Secretary of State Mathew Brown.

End

The Rhode Island Latino Civic Fund

Hereby confer this

Certificate of Achievement to

Melba Depena

 for successful completion of the Latina Institute Program and tireless devotion to the well-being of the Latino community of Rhode Island.

This 26th day of August Two Thousand Three

Melba Depena
President

Delia Rodriguez-Masjoan
Program Coordinator

Latina Leadership Institute 2005 Restructuring

Tomás Alberto Ávila

2005 Program Schedule

2005 Program Schedule

Activity	Date	Place	Presenter
Marketing Kick Off	December 10, 2005	Internet	
Official Application Available	January 1, 2005		
Application Deadline	January 31, 2005		
Applicants Interview Period	2/1 – 2/19 2005		
Applicants acceptance Notification	March 1st, 2005	Mail	
Official Kick Off	March 8th, 2005	State House	Anastacia Williams / Grace Diaz
Soy Mujer Breakfast	March 10, 2005	Ada's Creation	
Voter Registration Project	March 12, 2005	Central Falls	
Class Schedule			
1. Opening Class/Introduction	March 12, 2005	Community College of RI	Betty/Doris/Tomas
2. Getting to know our community	March 19, 2005	Knight Memorial, 275 Elmwood	Maria Martinez/Betty Bernal
3. Leadership Theory	March, 26 2005	Providence City Council	Pia Frye
4. Communication Skills	April 2, 2005	Johnson & Wales University	Richard Godfrey
5. Public Policy	April 9, 2005	American Cancer Society	Luis Aponte
6. Grass Root Activism	April 16, 2005	CHisRA	Shanah Kurland/Sarah Mersha
7. Boards & Commissions	April 23, 2005	Progreso Latino	Patricia/Martinez/Nellie Gorbea
8. Working with the media	April 30, 2005	PBS, Channel, Channel 36	Ana Cabrera
Graduation			
Latinos on the Hill	May 18, 2005	State House	
Campaign Training Workshop	May 21, 2005		
Women Suffrage Anniversary	August 26	Roger Williams Casino	
Central Falls Primary Elections	October 4	Central Falls	
Central Falls General Elections	November 1	Central Falls	

Potential Presenters
Cynthia Garcia-Coll
Kristine Peligrini
Rosa De Castillo
Betty Bernal
Lucia Gomez
Delia Rodriguez-Masjoan
Patricia Martinez
Maria Del Pilar
Abigail Mesa

Program Description

Program Purposes and Goals

The Latina Leadership Institute is committed to new paradigms of leadership, not in maintaining the status quo. As such, this program is for women who are ready for profound changes in their personal and professional lives. It will include deep, personal sharing and insights. In order to lead others, a leader must first know herself. "Knowing others is wisdom, knowing the self is enlightenment.

The Latina Leadership Institute program is an educational program. Distinguished leaders in the public and private sectors have recognized the excellence and relevance of Latina Leadership Institute's training program. Latina Leadership Institute's commitment, however, extends beyond helping Latina women succeed. The fellows are viewed by Latina Leadership Institute as agents of a much wider transformation.

The Latina Civic Fund has designed this institute with the purpose of providing hands on training for Latinas about community organizing, leadership skills, political involvement and advocacy. We are hoping to

The Latina Leadership Institute program provides 8-week leadership development-training sessions that span 3 months. The intensive learning experience provides training in public policy, leadership, strategic management, team building and race, class and gender issues. The program emphasizes a holistic approach to leadership. The LLI will select up to 30 Latinas per year with the following characteristics:
- Substantive professional work experience and significant direct accomplishments
- Current and potential leadership as indicated by professional, volunteer and other activities, as well as, through recommendations
- Strength of character, motivation and commitment to goals

The Latina Civic Fund will invite Latinas from across the state and our community socioeconomic demographics in an effort to promote leadership development among Latinas.

Latinas have been the backbone of the Latina community increasing civic participation within our state. These women often serve as volunteers in campaigns, coordinators of health fairs and other community involvement. Consequently, there is a dire need to formally provide guidance and information to these women who are involved at different levels of our community. The Latina community needs the tools to further develop Latinas in leadership positions, and be able to fully participate. We are excited about the opportunities that lie ahead for our community, and trust that this Leadership Institute will contribute to the overall improvement of our state.

Applicants must submit a complete application packet in order to be considered. Selection committee composed of Latina Leadership Institute Alumnae and members of the RI Latina Civic Fund schedule a personal or phone interview and submits their recommendation to the review committee.

Participation in Latina Leadership Institute requires involvement. Full attendance is required at all 8 educational sessions. Only one absence will be allowed for **emergency** purposes. A participant with more than two absences will not graduate from the program.

Vision

"Latinas as civic Leaders"

Mission

"To develop Latinas as civic leaders through training, professional development, relationship building, community and political activism."

Purpose

To ensure that Latina women develop their personal and professional potential to serve as leaders in their communities, move into greater leadership roles and advocate for positive changes in the Latina community.

Among Latina Leadership Institute's long-term goals are the following:

1. A strong and continuously growing network of Latina Leaders who play a key role in policy making throughout the state;

2. Increased Latina voter registration and voting rates;

3. Increased Latina involvement in electoral politics, and equitable representation among elected and appointed officials at both local and state levels;

4. Equitable Latina representation on mainstream nonprofit hoards and commissions

5. An organized Latina community demonstrating unity in its diversity, participating fully and actively in advocacy and public policy efforts throughout the state; and

6.
tronger, better-funded Latina community-based organizations with a strong sense of community accountability.

The organizers believe that Latina Leadership Institute can contribute to all these goals through leadership development that closely tied to the community and integrated with the organizers and the community's program and advocacy activities. The Latino Civic Fund has designed this institute with the purpose of providing hands on training for Latinas about community organizing, leadership skills, political involvement and advocacy.

Target Population

The Latina Leadership Institute targets participants that reflect the diverse racial and ethnic origins of the Rhode Island Latina community. The participants have diverse levels of educational, professional and personal experiences; all participants have to demonstrate a commitment to working for positive change within the Latina community. Currently based in Providence, it targets residents of various neighborhoods within or very near Providence; future cycles are expected to target Latinas in other cities within Rhode Island. The program is committed to including equal numbers of men and women.

The Leadership Program

Geared towards Latinas that show strong commitment to improving their community. The program goal is to foster active citizen participation in each of the participants. These sessions provide participants with information about accessing community resources prepare community members for decision-making roles and train them to become responsible and capable community advocates. At the end of this training, participants apply their skills by working actively with the Latina community

Components

The Latina Leadership Institute program provides 8-week leadership development-training sessions that span 3 months. The intensive learning experience provides training in public policy, leadership, strategic management, team building and race, class and gender issues. The program emphasizes a holistic approach to leadership. The LLI will select up to 30 Latinas per year with the following characteristics:
- Substantive professional work experience and significant direct accomplishments
- Current and potential leadership as indicated by professional, volunteer and other activities, as well as, through recommendations
- Strength of character, motivation and commitment to goals

The primary components have been fully implemented, although several supplemental components are operational Core components include organized skill-building seminars, committees and task forces, other structured activities, one major community project, regular associate meetings, supplemental activities arranged by Latina Leadership Institute staff to offer further opportunities for learning and community involvement, support services to reduce barriers to Latina Leadership Institute participation, and planned complementary and follow-up activities which have not been implemented. The following sections describe the purposes, methods, and experiences of these components.

Skills-Building Seminars

At the heart of Latina Leadership Institute are skills-building seminars designed to provide basic information and skill development in topic areas of broad use to individuals active in the community. Some focus on critical skills for associates such as organizing and negotiation skills, some provide important information such as steps in the legislative process, and still others provide practical skills such as how to run elections.

1. Community Organizing - Introduction and Basic Principles
2. Community Organizing - Campaign Development
3. Role of the Media in Grassroots Organizing
4. Negotiation Skills
5. The Legislative Process
6. Influencing Public Policy
7. Voting/Voter Education and Registration
8. Fundraising
9. Advocacy Skills
10. Running Effective Meetings

Latina Leadership Institute Components

Skills-Building Seminars

Sessions provided on Saturdays, to present and develop skills related to community involvement.

Committees and Task Forces

Structures used for community involvement; groups formed to reflect interests of associates, who learn about and advocate in relation to a specific program area; groups meet two or three times a month throughout the year and engage in a variety of community activities in group or in smaller task forces.

Other Structured Activities

Community forums and study circles used to address policy issues in an organized way; forums involve hearing multiple perspectives on an issue such as whether members of the school committee (the equivalent of school board) should be appointed or elected; study circles provide facilitated discussions of issues by the Latina Leadership Institute associates.

Community Project

One major group project during the year, designed to practice skills and benefit the community.

Associate Meetings

One meeting monthly of all associates, to report on group activities, share other information, and Latina Leadership Institute joint events.

Supplemental Activities

Access to conferences, training, involvement in advocacy coalitions, arranged by Latina Leadership Institute staff

> 1. Support Services - child care during sessions, breakfast and lunch during all-day sessions
>
> 2. Complementary Activities - newsletter, public policy interns to support the work of the Latina Leadership Institute associates.
>
> 3. Follow-Up Network - method for maintaining links among Latina Leadership Institute associates and encouraging their continued community involvement following graduation from the program (Latina Leadership Institute).

Training is held on Saturdays, with each session typically including 4-hour seminars. Seminars are interactive, typically including a combination of expert presentations of principles and examples, and hands-on skill-building exercises using case studies, problem-solving tasks, role-plays, or other active learning techniques. Usually, a seminar includes one or more outside facilitator's expert in the topic area.

In my opinion a high level of program participation is essential to create commitment and effective involvement, and that associates need the opportunity to develop a wide range of skills to support their community involvement. As a result, associates are now required to participate in one full day or training every month; very few absences arc permitted, and this arc usually "made up" through participation in some special activity.

Latina Leadership Institute will be providing training and background materials for each seminar,

Participation in Latina Leadership Institute requires involvement. Full attendance is required at all 8 educational sessions. Only one absence will be allowed for **emergency** purposes. A participant with more than two absences will not graduate from the program.

PROGRAM STRUCTURE

Week 1: General Introduction

- Introduction to program, expectations, orientation.
- Overview of Curriculum
- History of RI Latino Civic Fund
- Introduction of participants
- Latino Leaders: What have they achieved? What makes them unique?
- Community Leadership. What does it mean?

Week 2: Getting to know our Community

- Introduction to the needs of the local community
- Presentation by community activists
- Presentations by selected members of local agencies and advocacy groups and elected officials
- Group discussion: According to the participants, what are the true needs of the community and how can these needs be met?

Week 3: Leadership Theory

Leadership theory:
- Traits of effective leaders
- Leadership styles

Servant leadership
- What does it mean?
- Group discussion on servant leadership

Do participants see themselves as servant leaders?

Latino leadership:
- Discussion of Latino leadership concept and its meaning

- Issues of cultural identity and history will be addressed
- Discussion of standards placed on Latino leaders versus mainstream leaders.
- Who are some of the Latino leaders in Providence, in Rhode Island, and US?
- What contributions have they made to the community? State, and country

Week 4: Communication Skills

- Developing communication Skills
- Assertiveness:
    1. To learn to communicate your needs effectively
    2. Understand assertive and non-assertive behaviors
    3. Communication Philosophy and Theory

- Group discussion: Individual views on what constitutes effective communication skills and how they enhance person's leadership skills.

- Communication Skills
    1. Effective communication skills
    2. Effective listening skills
- Brainstorming & Public Speaking
    1. How to prepare and present a speech
    2. Addressing your audience.
    3. Public Speaking: Ten-minute speeches will be given on topics of choice.
    4. Group discussion: Participants will assess each other's public speaking strengths and
    5. Weaknesses

- How to run a meeting effectively
    1. Running a Meeting: Each participant will run a meeting for 10 minutes and try to achieve consensus on a particular issue

2. Group Discussion: Participants will access each other's strengths and weaknesses in running a meeting

Week 5: Public Policy

- What is Public Policy?
- The process of development, formulation and implementation of public policy
- Overview of local state system and structure

  - Health
  - Education
  - Economic
  - Personal Finance

- Group Project: Discussion of a pertinent community issue. How can an appropriate policy address this problem? What appropriate board, commission, or agency would be the most appropriate to implement such a policy?

Week 6: Grassroots Leadership and Activism

- Why should someone participate in grassroots activism?
- General guidelines for activism
- How to administer a letter writing campaign
- Basics of how to access and meet with politicians
- The dynamics of organizing grass root campaigns for voter education and registration.

Week 7. Introduction to Boards & Commissions

- Types of boards and their respective responsibilities
  - Corporate Boards
  - Private Boards

- o Public
- Characteristics of good Board members
- Roles of different Board members.
- Board ethics
- Understanding the responsibilities of serving on a board and the implicit accountability to the community.
  - Identify board and commissions which are important to the Providence Latino community
  - How to get placed on a board
  - How to advocate for board positions
  - How to build consensus on a board commission
  - Conclusion: Discussion on why Latinos need to serve on Boards that influence public policy.
  - Individual Projects: Each participant will do research about a local board, preferably a school board, and will write a brief summary of its latest projects, concerns and accomplishments. Each participant will discuss weather or not he/she would like to become part of the board and why? He/she will also discuss the strategies to follow if he/she wanted to be an appointed member of the board.

Week 8: Working With the Media

- How to write a press release
- How to get the media's attention
- How to make the media accountable to Latino Issues.
- How to develop a press kit.
- How to use statistics effectively
- How and where to research for sources of informational and statistical support

Campaign Training Workshop Agenda

Saturday, _____

8:00 – 8:45 a.m.   Registration & Continental Breakfast

8:45 – 9:00 a.m.   Welcome

9:00 – 10:30 a.m.   Developing a Campaign Plan

> (**Track I, Beginning/ Intermediate**) This session will provide participants with expert advice on putting together a campaign plan that includes: examining legal requirements, identifying the key organizational parts of the campaign team, developing a campaign timeline, and examining what it takes to run for office.
>
> Panelists:
>
>> **10:30 – 12:00 p.m.**   Workgroup Session I: "Developing Your Campaign Plan"
>
> (**Track I, Beginning/ Intermediate**) Participants will separate into workgroups where they will have an opportunity to work with a facilitator to put into practice the skills outlined in the previous general session.

9:00 – 10:30 p.m.   Rhode Island Numbers & Polling

> (**Track II, Advanced**) This session will provide participants with a demographic profile of the new districts in Rhode Island, utilizing 2000 census information as well as Polling information. The session will cover Rhode Island profile, demographics, statewide and local polling information, and issues analysis.
>
> Public Affairs Consultant
>
> Polling firm representative

10:30 – 12:00 noon   Media Skills Training

(**Tracks I & II**) Participants will learn how to deal with electronic and print press effectively, how to prepare a media alert, press release, and how to deliver message in thirty seconds with immediate feedback through role-playing exercises.

12:00 – 1:00 p.m.   Lunch

Keynote Lunch

1:00 – 2:00 p.m.   ABC's of Political Fundraising

(**Track I, Beginning/ Intermediate**) Participants will learn the building blocks to a successful political fundraising plan. They will learn about fundraising techniques, how to plan successful fundraising events and how to incorporate their fundraising plan into a budget.

2:00 – 3:00 p.m.   Workgroup Session II: "Putting Together a Fundraising Plan"

(**Track I, Beginning/ Intermediate**)   Participants will develop an outline for a fundraising plan. The exercise will require participants to raise $20,000 using at least ten different fundraising events through personal solicitation, fundraising committees, house parties, constituency groups, PACs, and large events. Participants will then place these events within a campaign timeline.

1:00 – 3:00 p.m.   Creating an Effective Mail Program

(**Track II, Advanced**) This session is designed help campaigns develop effective mail programs for campaigns. The session will cover how to combine the field operations with the mail program as well as how to maximize the mail program.

Political Strategist

3: 00 -3:15 pm   Break

3:15 – 4:30   Developing a Winning Campaign Message

(Track I, Beginning/ Intermediate) Participants will learn the fundamentals of developing an effective campaign message. Participants will begin by defining what a campaign message is, developing their own message, identifying the best vehicles to get out their message, and tailoring their message to various voters.

Panelists:

4:30 – 5:30 p.m. Workgroup Session I: "Developing Your Winning Campaign Message"

(Track I, Beginning/Intermediate) Participants will create a campaign message and begin to identify the various vehicles needed to deliver a winning message.

1:00 – 2:30 p.m.   Field Plan: Mobilizing for Victory

(Track I, Beginning/ Intermediate) Participants will learn the essentials to develop a successful field operation. This session will focus on developing effective field operations through identifying/targeting voters, door-to door canvassing, phone banking, recruiting/managing volunteers, GOTV techniques, and Election Day strategies.

December 20, 2005

Dear Applicant:

Thank you for your interest and support of the Latina Leadership Institute. Enclosed you will find the Latina Leadership Institute's application packet, including information that you or a candidate may find helpful in filling the application. By February, we will select approximately 30 Latinas to participate in the second Class of 2005.

The Latina Leadership Institute is committed to new paradigms of leadership, not in maintaining the status quo. As such, this program is for women who are ready for profound changes in their personal and professional lives. It will include deep, personal sharing and insights. In order to lead others, a leader must first know herself. "Knowing others is wisdom, knowing the self is enlightenment.

Benefits of participating in Latina Leadership Institute include:

- The opportunity to meet and work with other influential leaders from a diverse cross section of the state, developing many new contacts and relationships;
- Interactive and engaging sessions to enhance your capacity for leadership through training in group dynamics, public policy, leadership, strategic management, team building and race, class and gender issues; and
- Increased confidence, motivation, and commitment to becoming actively involved in promoting positive change across the state.

Feel free to pass on the enclosed information to anyone you would like to nominate for our 2005 Latina Institute. ***Applications are due by Friday, January 28 for the class beginning March 12 2005.***

If you have any questions, please contact Doris De Los Santos Program Coordinator or me at 401-274-5204.

Thank you again for your interest and support of Latina Leadership Institute.

Tomás A. Ávila
President

2005 APPLICATION INFORMATION

The Latina Leadership Institute is committed to new paradigms of leadership, not in maintaining the status quo. As such, this program is for women who are ready for profound changes in their personal and professional lives. It will include deep, personal sharing and insights. In order to lead others, a leader must first know her. "Knowing others is wisdom, knowing the self is enlightenment.

The Latina Leadership Institute program is an educational program. Distinguished leaders in the public and private sectors have recognized the excellence and relevance of the Latina Leadership Institute's training program. The Latina Leadership Institute's commitment, however, extends beyond helping Latino women succeed. The fellows are viewed by the Latina Leadership Institute as agents of a much wider transformation.

The Latino Civic Fund has designed this institute with the purpose of providing hands on training for Latinas about community organizing, leadership skills, political involvement and advocacy.

The Latina Leadership Institute program provides 8-week leadership development-training sessions which span 3 months. The intensive learning experience provides training in public policy, leadership, strategic management, team building and race, class and gender issues. The program emphasizes a holistic approach to leadership. The LLI will select up to 30 Latinas per year with the following characteristics:

- Substantive professional work experience and significant direct accomplishments
- Current and potential leadership as indicated by professional, volunteer and other activities, as well as, through recommendations
- Strength of character, motivation and commitment to goals

The Latino Civic Fund will invite Latinas from across the state and our community socioeconomic demographics to promote leadership development among Latinas.

Latinas have been the backbone of the Latino community increasing civic participation within our state. These women often serve as volunteers in campaigns, coordinators of health fairs and other community involvement. Consequently, there is a dire need to formally provide guidance and information to these women who are involved at different levels of our community. The Latino community needs the tools to further develop Latinas in leadership positions, and be able to fully participate. We are excited about the opportunities that lie ahead for our community, and trust that the Leadership Institute will contribute to the overall improvement of our state.

Applicants must submit a complete application packet in order to be considered. Selection committee composed of Latina Leadership Institute Alumnae and members of the RI Latino Civic Fund schedule a personal or phone interview with each applicant and submit their recommendation to the review committee.

Participation in Latina Leadership Institute requires involvement. Full attendance is required at all 8 educational sessions. Only one absence will be allowed for **emergency** purposes. A participant with more than two absences will not graduate from the program.

Latina Leadership Institute

2005 APPLICATION INFORMATION

As you prepare to complete the application for the 2005 Class of the Latina Leadership Institute, the following information is disclosed to provide you with a greater understanding of the program.

CRITERIA
The Latina Leadership Institute will select up to 30 Latinas per year with the following characteristics:

- Substantive professional work experience and significant direct accomplishments
- Current and potential leadership as indicated by professional, volunteer and other activities, as well as, through recommendations
- Strength of character, motivation and commitment to goals
- Intention to participate fully in all activities of the training, as well as, commitment to continue to support the Latina Leadership Institute
- The optimal candidate will have achieved success in her field, yet would benefit from this program.

SELECTION PROCESS

Applicants must submit a completed application packet in order to be considered. The Selection committee composed of Latina Leadership Institute Alumnae and members of the RI Latino Civic Fund schedule a personal or phone interview and submit their recommendation to the review committee. Up to 30 women from diverse professions, geographic areas and ethnic subgroups within the Latino community are selected and ***notified via mail or email by February 20, 2005***.

2005 SCHEDULE

The Latina Leadership Institute program kicks off March 8 with a ceremony at the State House in celebration of International Women Month. Beginning in March 12 and running through the end of April.

Class	Date
Opening Class/Introduction	March 12, 2005
Getting to know our community	March 19, 2005
Leadership Theory	March, 26 2005
Communication Skills	April 2, 2005
Public Policy	April 9, 2005
Grass Root Activism	April 16, 2005
Boards & Commissions	April 23, 2005
Working with the media	April 30, 2005

Latina Leadership Institute Application

PERSONAL

Date of Application: _____

Name: _____
    Last   First   Middle

Address: _____
    Street   City   State   Zip Code

Telephone: _____ Cell/Beeper: _____
_____ Email: _____

_____

DO YOU HAVE ANYPHYSICAL LIMITATIONS OR HANDICAPS REQUIRING SPECIAL ACCOMODATION?

How did you learn about the institute? _____

Date of Birth:_____Place of Birth:_____

Length of Residence in Rhode Island: _____

_____

In case of emergency notify: _____ Relationship: _____

Will you require Childcare services during the workshops? _____

Hobbies and Special Interest: _____

_____

_____

_____

_____

_____

_____

Check <u>one</u> of the following categories that best describes your present employment:

___ Business/Industry   ___ Labor   ___ Social Services   ___ Arts

___ Law   ___ Health   ___ Non Profit

___ Government   ___ Media

                         ___ Education   ___ Religion

        ___ Other

EMPLOYMENT

Present Employer: _____ Year Started _____

Type of Organization: _____

Title: _____

Since: _____

Briefly describe your current job responsibilities

_____
_____
_____
_____
_____
_____
_____
_____
_____
_____
_____

List previous employment in reverse chronological order – last position first.

Employer   **Title**

                   Period of Service

_____
_____
_____
_____
_____
_____
_____

Please list and briefly describe your three greatest strengths, and list and briefly describe your three areas for improvement.

_____
_____
_____
_____
_____
_____
_____
_____
_____
_____
_____
_____
_____

List any business/professional affiliations in which you are presently active or have been active.

Name of Organization   **Position Held**   **Period of Affiliation**

_____

_____

_____

_____

_____

EDUCATION

(Begin with high school, college(s), advanced degrees and/or specific training).

Name and Location of School   Dates (from-to)   Degree and Major

_____

_____

_____

_____

Leadership positions held:

_____

_____

_____

_____

_____

COMMUNITY INVOLVEMENT

Please list up to three important community, religious or civic activities in which you have participated in the past five years. Indicate your level/type of involvement.

Organization   **Position Held**   **Period of Affiliation**

_____

_____

_____

_____

_____

What do you consider to be the five most important qualities or characteristics of a leader?

Please explain what you consider to be your most important accomplishment in one of the above organizations. How did you exhibit a leadership role?

What kind of leadership roles would you like to be carrying out five to ten years from now? Be as specific as possible.

Do you believe Latina leaders are different from other leaders? If yes, how? If no, why not?

LATINO COMMUNITY PERSPECTIVE

The Latino community faces many socioeconomic, cultural and political challenges. Identify one policy area of particular interest to you (i.e. immigration, education, health care, employment, etc.) and summarize 3-4 important aspects pertaining to this policy area that impact the Latino community.

_____
_____
_____
_____
_____
_____

Describe what you believe needs to happen at the policy, program and/or community levels to address the issues you have identify.

_____
_____
_____
_____
_____

What are your short-term professional and personal goals? What is your plan for achieving them? (List up to three.) Where would you like to be three to five years from now? What are your long-term professional and personal goals?

_____
_____
_____
_____

If selected for this program, what unique contributions would you bring to Latina Leadership Institute? and
what has been your greatest contribution to the advancement of Latino women?

_____
_____
_____
_____
_____
_____

GENERAL INFORMATION

Give any other information you feel would be helpful to the Selection Committee in evaluating your application.

_____

_____

_____

Have you applied to Latina Leadership Institute in the past? ___ Yes ___ No   If yes, what year?_____

How did you become interested in Latina Leadership Institute? ___ LLI Graduate Referral ___ News Articles ___ LLI Advertisement ___ Other_____

COMMITMENT

The program goal is to foster active citizen participation in each of the graduates of the Latina Leadership Institute. This is accomplished through the sessions that provide participants with information about accessing community resources prepare community alumni for decision-making roles and train them to become responsible and capable community advocates. At the end of this training, participants are expected to apply their skills by working actively constructive community change.

You are also encouraged to serve on committees. Boards. and to participate in organizations throughout the state. Alumni have the responsibility to ensure perpetuation of active leadership in the state: and therefore, are expected to support the work of the Latina Leadership Institute.

APPLICANT'S COMMITMENT

I certify that all information and statements in this application are true and correct to the best of my knowledge. I understand that the information in this application may be verified. If selected, I will participate in **all** training sessions, contribute to the best of my ability, mentor two Latino women and complete a leadership project as a part of my commitment to the Latina Leadership Institute.

_____
SIGNATURE:

_____
Name & Title (print)

_____
DATE

SUBMIT:COMPLETED APPLICATION by 5:00 PM JANUARY 28, 2005

Latina Leadership Institute
C/o Tomás Á
Tomas Avila
61 Tappan Street, Suite 1
Providence, RI 02908
or
Email to: latinocivicfund@yahoo.com

Campaign Training Application

Name _____
Address _____
City _____
State _____ **Zip** _____
Phone: **Home** _____ **Work** _____
Fax _____
Email _____

_____
School/University _____

Please tell us about previous campaign experience:
None_____   Senatorial_____
Municipal_____   Statewide_____
State House/Senate_____   Coordinated Campaign_____
Congressional_____   Presidential_____

Please complete the following for each campaign:
Name of campaign_____

Position or title_____
Duties and Responsibilities_____

_____
Dates of campaign work_____ Victory: Y___ N___

Name of campaign_____

Position or title_____

Duties and Responsibilities_____

Dates of campaign work_____ Victory Y___ N___

Name of campaign_____

Position or title_____

Duties and Responsibilities_____

Dates of campaign work_____
Victory Y_ N_

Rank your abilities/experience in each of the following areas:

Campaign Activities	Extensive	Some	Little	None
Voter Registration				
Field Operations				
Message development				
Media Relations				
Fundraising				
Campaign Management				

1. Are you currently affiliated with a campaign? If so, for how long and in what position?
2. Are you or do you plan on being a candidate for public office? If so please explain.
3. What are you hoping to learn from participating in the campaign training?

Marketing
Press Release

January 1, 2005

For Immediate Release

Contact: Doris De Los Santos
401-123-4567

Latina Leadership Institute is now accepting applications for its 2005 Class

The Rhode Island Latino Civic Fund is now accepting applications for its 2005 Latina Leadership Institute. The Latina Leadership Institute provides the opportunity to meet and work with other emerging and influential Latina leaders from a diverse cross section of the state, developing new contacts and relationships; engaging sessions to enhance your capacity for leadership through training in public policy, leadership, strategic management, team building and race, class and gender issues; and Increased confidence, motivation, and commitment to becoming actively involved in promoting positive change across the state.

The institute plans to provide eight sections for 4 hours each to start March 12, 2005. Applications will be available January 3rd. 2005 and will be due back by January 31st, 2005. The Latino Civic Fund will invite Latinas from across the state and our community socioeconomic demographics in an effort to promote leadership development among Latinas.

The Latina Leadership Institute is committed to new paradigms of leadership, not in maintaining the status quo. As such, this program is for women who are ready for profound changes in their personal and professional lives. It will include deep, personal sharing and insights. In order to lead others, a leader must first know herself. "Knowing others is wisdom, knowing the self is enlightenment.

The Latina Leadership Institute program is an educational program. Distinguished leaders in the public and private sectors have recognized the excellence and relevance of Latina Leadership Institute's training program. Latina Leadership Institute's commitment, however, extends beyond helping Latino women succeed. The fellows are viewed by Latina Leadership Institute as agents of a much wider transformation.

To apply send your name, organization, address, phone and email to RI Latino Civic latinocivicfund@yahoo.com or Doris De Los Santos goroi@cox.net or fax to 401-633-6535

Date: Tue, 14 Dec 2004 14:21:10 -0800 (PST)
From: "RI Latino Civic Fund" <latinocivicfund@yahoo.com>
View Contact Details
Subject: Latina Leadership Institute is now accepting applications
To: Anamaria2412@aol.com

Latina Leadership Institute is now accepting applications for its 2005 ClassThe Rhode Island Latino Civic Fund is now accepting applications for its 2005 Latina Leadership Institute. This statewide program provides a leadership-training environment for emerging Latina leaders. It also provides an opportunity for Latina leaders from diverse backgrounds to forge relationships and networks that will benefit themselves and the community throughout their careers.

The Latino Civic Fund has designed this institute with the purpose of providing hands on training for Latinas about community organizing, leadership skills, political involvement and advocacy.

We are planning to provide eight sections for 4 hours each section. The Latino Civic Fund will invite Latinas from across the state, housewives, and community leaders in an effort to promote leadership development among Latinas.

To apply send your name, organization (if any), address, phone and email to RI Latino Civic latinocivicfund@yahoo.com, Betty Bernal Betty.Bernal@cancer.org or Doris De Los Santos goroi@cox.net or fax to 633-6535

December 17, 2004

Latina Leadership Institute is now accepting applications for its 2005 Class

The Rhode Island Latino Civic Fund is now accepting applications for its 2005 Latina Leadership Institute. The Latina Leadership Institute provides the opportunity to meet and work with other emerging and influential Latina leaders from a diverse cross section of the state, developing new contacts and relationships; engaging sessions to enhance your capacity for leadership through training in public policy, leadership, strategic management, team building and race, class and gender issues; and Increased confidence, motivation, and commitment to becoming actively involved in promoting positive change across the state.

The Latina Leadership Institute is committed to new paradigms of leadership, not in maintaining the status quo. As such, this program is for women who are ready for profound changes in their personal and professional lives. It will include deep, personal sharing and insights. In order to lead others, a leader must first know herself. "Knowing others is wisdom, knowing the self is enlightenment.

The Latina Leadership Institute program is an educational program. Distinguished leaders in the public and private sectors have recognized the excellence and relevance of Latina Leadership Institute's training program. Latina Leadership Institute's commitment, however, extends beyond helping Latino women succeed. The fellows are viewed by Latina Leadership Institute as agents of a much wider transformation.

To apply send your name, organization (if any), address, phone and email to RI Latino Civic latinocivicfund@yahoo.com, Betty Bernal betty.Bernal@cancer.org or Doris De Los Santos goroi@cox.net or fax to 633-6535

Invitation Letter

Thank you for your interest and support of the Latina Leadership Institute. Enclosed you will find the Latina Leadership Institute's application packet, including information that you or a candidate may find helpful. By February, we will select approximately 30 Latinas to participate in the second Class of 2005.

The Latina Leadership Institute is committed to new paradigms of leadership, not in maintaining the status quo. As such, this program is for women who are ready for profound changes in their personal and professional lives. It will include deep, personal sharing and insights. In order to lead others, a leader must first know herself. "Knowing others is wisdom, knowing the self is enlightenment.

Benefits of participating in Latina Leadership Institute include:
- The opportunity to meet and work with other influential leaders from a diverse cross section of the state, developing many new contacts and relationships;
- Interactive and engaging sessions to enhance your capacity for leadership through training in group dynamics, public policy, leadership, strategic management, team building and race, class and gender issues; and
- Increased confidence, motivation, and commitment to becoming actively involved in promoting positive change across the state.

Feel free to pass on the enclosed information to anyone you would like to nominate for our 2005 Latina Institute. ***Applications are due by Friday, January 28 for the class beginning March 12 2005.***

If you have any questions, please contact Doris De Los Santos Program Coordinator or me at 401-123-4567.

Thank you again for your interest and support of Latina Leadership Institute.

Tomas Alberto Avila
President

Latina Leadership Institute Presenters Letter
New Immigrants, New Empowerment, New Leaders

January 1, 2005

Dear Friend/Colleague:

We take this opportunity to inform you that you have been nominated to be a presenter in the our 2005 Latina Leadership Institute to be held in Providence, Rhode Island on March 12 – May 30, 2005. The institute will bring together 30 Latinas from across the state, housewives, and community leaders in an effort to promote leadership development among Latinas. This statewide program provides a leadership-training environment for emerging Latina leaders and provides an opportunity for Latina leaders from diverse backgrounds to forge relationships and networks that will benefit themselves and the community throughout their careers.

You have been nominated to be a presenter in the **Education Empowerment Workshop** schedule to take place on MM/DD/YY at _____, Rhode Island 9:00 AM – 2:00 PM.

We hope that you will accept our invitation and honor us with your presence at this important event for the Latino community and the state. If you accept this invitation, please fill out the attached form and return it as soon as possible (and no later than MM/DD/YY). This will ensure your acceptance of our invitation.

Your participation in this event will be an investment in the well being of all Latinas. We look forward to your response and anticipate seeing you on the above date. For more information, please call.

Sincerely,

_____
Tomás A. Avila
President

Reference

February 26, 2003

Simone P. Joyaux
The Women's Fund of Rhode Island
One Union Station
Providence, RI 02903

Dear Ms. Joyaux:

The Latina Leadership Institute is delighted to submit this Letter of Intent to be considered for the Women's Fund Grant. We are excited about coordinating the first Annual Latina Political Symposium 2005 and hope that you can give us the opportunity to submit a full proposal.

Organization Mission Statement:
The Latina Leadership Institute is committed to promoting the participation of Latinas in leadership positions through hands-on training, professional and leadership development, political participation and voluntarism.

Project Description:
The Latina Political Symposium is an idea that emerged during our first-year evaluation of the Latina Leadership Institute. During the Institute the participants expressed an interest in further evaluating Latina Political participation. The project will include 3 modules:

- Voter Registration and Voter Education: This is developed to encourage Latinas to register to vote while promoting the need to learn about the political process of the state.

❑ Political Training: This is designed to assist any women who may be interested in running for office or coordinating a campaign.

❑ Political Activism: This is designed to motivate Latinas to continue involved in the political system by becoming volunteers.

Latinas have been the backbone of the Latino community's increasing civic participation within our state. These women serve as volunteers in campaigns, as coordinators at health fairs and many more community activities. Consequently, there is a dire need to formally provide guidance and information so they can utilize these new skills to better serve the community at different levels of our community.

Latinas need the tools to further develop knowledge, skills and abilities that will place them into leadership positions, and actively participate in all sector of the community. We are excited about all the wonderful opportunities that lie ahead for our community, and trust that this first Annual Latina Political Symposium will contribute to the overall improvement of our state.

The Women's fund of Rhode Island has a strong commitment to providing women equal access to opportunities in social, economic, education and political aspects. We are certain that the Annual Latina Political Symposium will serve as catalyst through which this can be accomplished.

Please feel free to contact us. Thank you for considering our request.

Sincerely,

Melba Depena   Delia Rodriguez Masjoan
721-9900   462-0524

The Rhode Island Latino Civic Fund

The Rhode Island Latino Civic Fund was organized in 2001 and operated for the purposes of promoting civic values and social welfare within the meaning of Section 501(c)(4) of the Internal Revenue Code of 1986, as amended. Our mission is to facilitate the incorporation of members of the Latino community into the American civic mainstream and to help them develop the skills that lead to civic participation. The Rhode Island Latino Civic Fund is a nonpartisan, nonprofit organization formed to advance the following goals:

- To promote the participation of the Latino community in the civic life and democratic processes of Rhode Island through activities such as those that increase voter education, voter registration and voter participation.

- To raise awareness in the Latino community regarding public policy issues benefiting Latinos and other individuals from urban communities as well as those that could adversely impact the Latino community.

The growth of the Latino population in Rhode Island during the last three decades, and the lack of existing state civic education organizations to adequately serve the needs of this population, led to the incorporation of the agency in 2001. Local Hispanic leaders established the non-profit agency to be directed and staffed by bilingual/bicultural Latino individuals to address the civic needs of the growing Latino community. We have a majority female and predominantly Hispanic board of directors composed of local community members from different Latin American countries.

During the 2002 election season, the Civic Fund witnessed the continuation of a number of trends in Latino voting behavior. The first was the sustained upward trajectory of Latino registration and voting that was dramatically underlined by an increase of close to 8,000 Latino votes cast from 1996. This fact about the Latino vote in 2000 has been widely reported, and is generally known. What is less well known, is that this increase in Latino votes has been accomplished through grass roots efforts that were endangered by the redistricting plan approved by the Rhode Island Legislature. The Rhode Island Latino Civic Fund, plays a crucial role in educating and registering Latinos to exercise their vote, and in partnership with other organizations mobilized the community during the elections.

In 2003, Rhode Island Latino Civic Fund became a recipient of a state Legislative grant to establish The Latino Voter Registration Project established to promote the civic participation of Latinos in South Side of Providence, where the largest Hispanic population of the state resides. The Latino Civic Fund in collaboration with the Latino Voting Rights Coalition of Rhode Island administers the program. This project established the framework and a comprehensive civic and voter education strategy to mobilize the Latino community for increased participation and turnout at elections during the present election period.

The organization's strengths lies in its committed volunteer membership and Board of Directors that have dedicated their time and financial resources, as well as their extensive diverse network to the benefit of the Latino community. The organization strength also lies in the experienced developed through the civic empowerment of members of the Board of Directors through their efforts in the Rhode Island Latino Political Action Committee that preceded the Rhode Island Latino Civic Fund in 1998.

Challenges and Opportunities

The Hispanic electorate is emerging as a distinct presence on the civic participation landscape, demonstrating broad but shallow party loyalty and a mixture of ideological beliefs and policy positions that defies easy categorization. At a time when the rest of the nation is almost evenly split along partisan lines, Latino voters appear to straddle some of the sharpest divides in American politics today. This represent an opportunity for the Rhode Island Latino Civic Fund with an increased opportunity to fulfill its mission, to facilitate the incorporation of members of the Latino community into the American civic mainstream and to help them develop the skills that lead to civic participation. The members of the organization believe that all of us, as Hispanics and as Americans, share a vital obligation: to participate and participate effectively in the civic participation process.

Research shows that, despite significant progress, Hispanics have a long way to go to achieve full equity in our civic participation. The challenge we face today is qualitatively different than that faced by our forefathers. From immigration to education, our community finds itself in a politically hostile environment, having to defend ourselves on even the most basic of civil rights. According to the Pew Hispanic Institute: the majority (71%) of Latinos, who are U.S. citizens but are not registered to vote, were born in the United States and over eight in ten (82%) speak English as a primary language (including 35% who are bilingual). One-third of the Hispanic population is currently applying for citizenship (9%) or plans to apply (24%).

Through the "Vota Latino" campaign a statewide non-partisan mobilization effort aimed at increasing voter participation in areas where Latinos and other ethnic minorities are concentrated, the Rhode Island Latino Civic Fund plans to incorporate the participation and involvement of the Latino community by focusing on civic education campaigns aimed at young, low-income, and recently registered voters. The campaign will register voters in centers of commerce; education, worship and entertainment across highly populate Latino districts followed by Get-Out-And-Vote efforts targeting newly registered Latino voters as well as occasional voters.

2005 Activities Calendar

The Latina Leadership Institute — March 12
The Latina Leadership Institute is committed to new paradigms of leadership, not in maintaining the status quo. As such, this program is for women who are ready for profound changes in their personal and professional lives. It will include deep, personal sharing and insights. In order to lead others, a leader must first know herself. "Knowing others is wisdom, knowing the self is enlightenment. The Latina Leadership Institute program is an educational program.

Soy Mujer: Latinas Past, Present & Future — March 17
The Soy Mujer! Breakfast is schedule to take place Thursday March 17 to commemorate International Women's Day and Women's History Month and to bring awareness of the impact Latino women have made on the world. International Women's Day is celebrated worldwide each year on March 8. As set forth by the United Nations General Assembly, the main reasons for celebrating International Women's Day are to recognize that peace and social progress require the active participation and equality of women and to acknowledge the contribution of women to international peace and security.

Latinos On the Hill — May 18
Latino Day in the State House will be an opportunity for elected officials to establish a closer relationship with the Latino community. The event gives Latinos an opportunity to come to the State House during a session of the General Assembly, and to meet with their local legislators to promote our legislative priorities.

The day will begin either in the House or Senate gallery. Participants will have a chance to observe the opening of the sessions, listen to the debate on the floor, and take note of the votes on various bills. Legislators say that they rely heavily on the viewpoints of their constituents when deciding, and welcome more of their input. By visiting the State House, and participating in a day of observations and meetings, both formal and informal, Latinos can effectively voice our issues and the public policies needed for the growth of our community.

Voter registration campaign
The Rhode Island Latino Civic Fund (RILCF) will conduct nonpartisan voter registration campaign during three windows of time: Winter-Spring 2004, Summer-Fall 2005. The **"Tu Voto es Tu Voz"** Campaign will register voters in centers of commerce, education, worship and entertainment.

For more information about the activities, contact the Latino Civic Fund @ latinocivicfund@yahoo.com or **401-274-5204**

Latina Leadership Class Puts Emphasis On Social Advocacy, Political Involvement

David Casey
Pawtucket Times
01/04/2005

PROVIDENCE -- The Latina Leadership Institute's fourth annual leadership class is coming to Central Falls, Pawtucket and Providence in 2005.

The Institute, a program of The Rhode Island Latino Civic Fund, is currently accepting applications from a new batch of ambitious, upward-mobile Latinas from every corner of the Ocean State.

The idea behind the Institute is simple, according to **President Tomás Alberto Ávila**: prepare Latinas for political leadership and social advocacy roles and, in doing so, increase political representation and social opportunity for Latinas -- burning the candle of gender and ethnic disparity at both ends, as it were.

In a related statement issued on New Year's Day, RILCF noted that the "Latina Leadership Institute's commitment ...extends beyond helping Latino women succeed. The fellows are viewed by The Latina Leadership Institute as agents of a much wider transformation."

The Institute will host eight four-hour classes in each of the aforementioned cities starting on March 12.

Latinas of all ages and socio-economic backgrounds are invited to enroll, free of charge, by Jan. 28.

The Institute's curriculum is geared toward leadership development, networking, and mentoring and community involvement.

Students will have the opportunity to hobnob with established and up- and- coming Latina leaders (this year's faculty includes Central Falls resident **Carmen Mirabel**, Section 8 director with the Rhode Island

Housing and Mortgage Finance Corporation) while learning about public policy, leadership theory, strategic management, team building, political campaigning, public speaking, media relations and -- of course -- the myriad racial, class and gender issues facing the state's mushrooming Latina population.

Progreso Latino Executive Director **Edwin Cancel**, whose Central Falls-based organization will host classes this year, hailed the Institute as a valuable resource for local Latinas.

"There are not a lot of Latinas in political leadership roles in Rhode Island, and I think that any program that helps with skill development and encourages networking is good for our community," he said.

In 2002 the Women's Fund of Rhode Island, a subset of the Rhode Island Foundation, published "The Status of Women in Rhode Island," a statistical study of women's relative health, economic success and political activity in the Ocean State.

Ávila and his RILCF colleagues were surprised to learn that female Rhode Islanders exhibited some of the lowest levels of political participation and representation in the country.

Ávila would soon discover that Rhode Island's Latinas were much worse-off than their white counterparts.

The problem and its ostensible solution, the prototypical Latina Leadership Institute, crystallized when RILCF considered another sign of Latina detachment: a steady stream of requests for Latina board members, commissioners and councilors from a wide array of public and private organizations.

Latinas interested in enrolling should send their name, organization (if applicable), address, phone and e-mail address to RILCF at latinocivicfund@yahoo.com or Doris De Los Santos at goroi@cox.net or by fax at 633-6535.

Latina Institute Graduates 17 Leaders

The program is aimed at young women who have a background in public service, education and government.

By Linda Borg
Journal Staff Writer
Tuesday, May 31, **2005**

PROVIDENCE -- Patricia Martinez, the interim director of the state Department of Children, Youth and Families, was honored last week at the graduation of 17 women from the Rhode Island Latina Leadership Institute.

The graduates chose Martinez because she has been a pioneer for Latino women in civic participation and leadership in the community, according to Ana-Cecelia Rosado, a member of the Rhode Island Latino Civic Fund, which sponsors the classes.

The speaker was **Melba De Pena**, the executive director of the state Democratic Party.

The Civic Fund, which graduated its second class, originally asked 22 women to participate in an eight-week training program where they learned about leadership skills, grass-roots advocacy, media relations and the workings of government and media relations.

The group's mission is to "ensure that Latino women develop their personal and professional potential to serve as leaders in their communities and advocate for positive changes in the Latino community," said **Doris M. De Los Santos, vice president of the Civic Fund.**

Carmen A. Mirabal, coordinator of the Leadership Institute, said that she was "very proud to say that these . . . successful Latinas have the communication and motivational skills, the personal courage, the integrity and the honesty necessary to guide the Latino community."

The program, which runs for eight weeks on Saturdays, is aimed at young women with a background in public service, education and government who are interested in assuming a more prominent role in their community. The institute was created to address the large gender gap between Latino men and women who hold positions of influence.

The classes are sponsored by Sodexho School Services, the Neighborhood Health Plan of Rhode Island, Mayor David N. Ciciline's office and the Rhode Island Foundation.

The following women graduated Thursday:

Yolanda Baez

Evelyn Castillo

Martha Cedeño

Rosa Q. Crowley

Cynthia DeJesus

Irisonixa Diaz

Diana Figueroa

Judelkys García

Alma Guzmán

Judith Koegler

Katia Lugo

Olinda Matos

Vivian Moreno

Sonja Ogando

Patricia Patterson

Rosemary Raygada

Silvia Reyes.

2006 LLI

1. Ana Rivas
2. Arelis Valerio
3. Beiyanil Pena
4. Benita Chang de Santiago
5. Bety Huaranga
6. Cannen Morales
7. Carolina Briones
8. Dulce Hernandez
9. Esperanza Gomez
10. Gaby Molina
11. Gloria Rojas
12. Altabeiry Jorge
13. Jovanna Garcia
14. Lillyarn del Carmen Tabares
15. Lubia Garcia
16. Ludys Cortorreal
17. Maria Cotto
18. Maria Aguilar
19. Maria Fajardo
20. Mendrid Peralta

1. Mildred Rodriguez
2. Mirna Calderon
3. Nazly Guzman-Singletary
4. Olga Granados
5. Paola Harris
6. Raisa Burgos
7. Raysa Marte
8. Ruth Fuerte
9. Tania Quezada
10. Viviana Knowles
11. Xiomara Rodriguez
12. Yasmin Rincon
13. Zoila Bernal

LLI 2007

Congratulations to Obed Papp LLI 2007

LLI 2008

Congratulations to Carmen Diaz-Jusino LLI 2008

Congratulations to Carmen Diaz-Jusino for being named one of this year's YWCA Rhode Island Women of Achievement!

Carmen Diaz Jusino has been with the Center for Women & Enterprise, for the past eight years. She has a diverse array of professional experience – educator, community resources representative, job developer, counselor for teenagers, Spanish interpreter and manager. Jusino is also an entrepreneur having started a learning center in her home country, the Dominican Republic. Today she is the director of New Enterprise and WBC, for CWE's four locations in New England. She holds degrees in Social Studies and Psychology and a Master in Science-Concentration in Organizational Management and Leadership.

I'd Strongly Recommend Ladies This Free Leadership Institute With RI Latino Civic Fund.

I'm An Alumni From Class Of 2008 And Was One Of The Best Things I Invested Time Into!!! Jessica Thigpen, March 19, 2013

2009 LLI

 **Jovanna Garcia**
August 21, 2014

Toda una Leader Latina! 2009 LLI Class

2010 LLI

2011 LLI

El grupo de graduandas de la Clase 2011 del Instituto de Liderazgo para Latinas.

Instituto de Liderazgo celebra Graduación de su Clase 2011

El acto fue realizado en el Casino del Parque Roger Williams y contó con la presencia de líderes comunitarios, representantes, funcionarios y otros invitados especiales.

Por Anibis Peña Brito
PROVIDENCE EN ESPAÑOL

PROVIDENCE.- Con los auspicios del Rhode Island Latino Civic Fund, el Instituto de Liderazgo (LLI) celebró la Ceremonia de Graduación de su Clase 2011 en la que investió como líderes a 15 mujeres hispanas de distintas nacionalidades.

El acto de graduación fue realizado en el Casino del Parque Roger Williams y contó con la presencia de líderes comunitarios, representantes estatales, funcionarios, entre otros invitados especiales.

Las graduandas fueron Lisselle Carmona, Paula Choquette, Marcia De Jesús, Josefina Díaz, Miguelina Domínguez, Melida Espinal, Elizabeth Fernández, Magali García, Lissette Guzmán, Meisy Parisete, Karina Peláez, Auria Sánchez, Iris Silva, Magira Valentiner y Natalia Zapata.

Las palabras de bienvenida estuvieron a cargo de Carmen Díaz-Jusino, coordinadora del Programa de Liderazgo para Latinas, quien destacó la dedicación de las graduandas para aprovechar al máximo las enseñanzas recibidas en diversas áreas, todas con el objetivo de promover cambios positivos en la comunidad.

"Su participación en el Latina Leadership Institute es solo el comienzo para estas mujeres, un punto de partida que les ayudará a entender cómo llegar a ser líderes comprometidas y con sentido de la ética. El Instituto confía en que ellas sean modelos a seguir en los años venideros", expresó Díaz-Jusino.

La ceremonia de graduación tuvo como oradora principal a la señora Carmen Aguilar, quien se refirió a los diferentes roles que desempeña la mujer a lo largo de su vida, en tanto que Olga Noguera, pionera en el trabajo comunitario en Rhode Island, exhortó a las futuras líderes a involucrarse en labores que contribuyan al mejoramiento de su comunidad, citando como ejemplo los aportes legados por Juanita Sánchez, María Luisa Vallejo, entre otras hispanas destacadas.

A nombre de las graduandas dieron las palabras de agradecimiento Magali García, en español y Melida Espina, en inglés. Ambas explicaron el trabajo comunitario que más les gusta y en el que piensan encaminar esfuerzos para impulsar los cambios necesarios. Las áreas en las que se sienten identificadas son educación, salud, pequeña empresa, superación personal, orientación familiar, entre otras.

Durante la ceremonia, la clase del 2011 entregó una placa de reconocimiento al Comité Coordinador del programa de LLI, "por toda su dedicación y compromiso de tiempo, apoyo e inspiración para las mujeres de nuestra comunidad", galardón que fue recibido por la coordinadora Carmen Díaz-Jusino.

Como es tradición cada año, el LLI entregó el "Latina Leadership Award", un premio a una líder latina destacada en su comunidad, reconocimiento que en esta ocasión recayó en la Concejal Sabina Matos, graduada del Programa de Liderazgo en la promoción del 2003, y quien expresó su agradecimiento por la distinción conferida.

Además de sus certificados de participación en el Programa de Liderazgo, las graduandas de la Clase 2011 recibieron "citations" de la oficina del gobernador Lincoln Chafee, del Vice gobernador Elizabeth Roberts, los senadores Jack Reed y Sheldon Whitehouse, el congresista David Cicilline, la tesorera del Estado, Gina Raimondo, la representante Grace Díaz, así como de los alcaldes de Providence y Pawtucket Ángel Taveras y Donald Grebien respectivamente.

El LLI ha sido creado en 2003, por iniciativa del RI Latino Civic Fund, con el objetivo de impulsar la formación de un liderazgo femenino emergente dentro de la comunidad. Líderes de los sectores públicos y privados reconocen la relevancia del programa de entrenamiento desarrollado por el Instituto.

El programa de formación se prolonga por cuatro meses con varias sesiones de trabajo en las que se enfrenta a las participantes en áreas de políticas públicas, superación personal, liderazgo, temas de salud que afectan a la mujer, voluntariado, manejo de estrategias, relaciones con los medios de comunicación, oratoria, defensoría, trabajo en equipo, asuntos de género, entre otras.

Las futuras líderes tienen lo propio también de conducir trabajos en equipo que resulten en proyectos de investigación en los que se identifican los problemas que afectan o a la comunidad latina en Rhode Island, conjuntamente con recomendaciones y posibles soluciones para cada una de las temas identificadas. Este año los proyectos versaron sobre temas de educación, salud y migración.

Forman parte también del Comité Coordinador del Programa de Líderes Latinas Doris Blanchard, Grace González, Osmany Rodríguez, Norelys Consuegra, Francia Pacheco y Vianela Núñez.

El RI Latino Civic Fund fue fundado en 2002 con la misión de promover la participación de la comunidad latina en la vida cívica y los procesos democráticos del estado de Rhode Island, a través de actividades como educación y registro para votantes, participación en procesos electorales y desarrollo de liderazgo.

Las graduandas entregaron una placa de reconocimiento al Comité Coordinador del Programa de formación de Líderes Latinas.

Norelys Consuegra hace entrega del "Latina Leadership Award 2011" a la Concejal Sabina Matos.

Instituto de Liderazgo celebra Graduación de su Clase 2011

El acto fue realizado en el Casino del Parque Roger Williams y contó con la presencia de líderes comunitarios, representantes, funcionarios y otros invitados especiales.

Por Arelis Peña Brito
Providence En Español

Instituto de Liderazgo celebra Graduación de su Clase 2011

PROVIDENCE.- Con los auspicios del Rhode Island Latino Civic Fund, el Instituto de Liderazgo (LLI) celebró la Ceremonia de Graduación de su Clase 2011 en la que invistió como líderes a **15** mujeres hispanas de distintas nacionalidades. El acto de graduación fue realizado en el Casino del Parque Roger Williams y contó con la presencia de líderes comunitarios, representantes estatales, funcionarios, entre otros invitados especiales.

El acto de graduación fue realizado en el Casino del Parque Roger Williams y contó con la presencia de líderes comunitarios, representantes estatales, funcionarios, entre otros invitados especiales.

Las graduandas fueron:
Lissette Carmona
Paula Choquette
Marcia De Jesús
Josefina Días
Miguelina Domínguez
Mélida Espinal
Elizabeth Fernández
Magali García
Lissette Guzmán
Mercy Parada
Karina Peláez
Aura Sánchez
Iris Silva
Magira Valentiner
Natalia Zapata

Las palabras de bienvenida estuvieron a cargo de **Carmen Díaz-Jusino, coordinadora del Programa** de Liderazgo para Latinas, quien destacó la dedicación de las graduandas para aprovechar al máximo las enseñanzas recibidas en diversas áreas, todas con el objetivo común de promover cambios positivos en la comunidad.

"Su participación en el Latina Leadership Institute es solo el comienzo para estas mujeres, un punto de partida que les ayudará a entender cómo llegar a ser líderes comprometidas y con sentido de la ética. El Instituto confía en que ellas serán modelos a seguir en los años venideros", expresó DíazJusino.

La ceremonia de graduación tuvo como oradora principal a la señora Carmen Aguilar, quien se refirió a los diferentes roles que desempeña la mujer a lo largo de su vida; en tanto que Olga Noguera, pionera en el trabajo comunitario en Rhode Island, exhortó a las futuras líderes a involucrarse en labores que contribuyan al mejoramiento de su comunidad, citando como ejemplo los aportes legados por Juanita Sánchez, María Luisa Vallejo, entre otras hispanas destacadas.

A nombre de las graduandas dieron las palabras de agradecimiento **Magali García**, en español; y **Mélida Espinal**, en inglés. Ambas explicaron el trabajo comunitario que más les gusta y en el que piensan encaminar esfuerzos para impulsar los cambios necesarios. Las áreas con las que se sienten identificadas son educación, salud, pequeña empresa, superación personal, orientación familiar, entre otras.

Durante la ceremonia, la clase del 2011 entregó una placa de reconocimiento al Comité Coordinador del programa del LLI, "por toda su dedicación y compromiso de tiempo, apoyo e inspiración para las mujeres de nuestra comunidad", galardón que fue recibido por la coordinadora Carmen Díaz-Jusino.

Como es tradición cada año, el LLI entregó **el "Latina Leadership Award"**, un premio a una líder latina destacada en su comunidad, reconocimiento que en esta oportunidad recayó en la Concejal Sabina Matos, graduada del Programa de Liderazgo en la promoción del 2003, y quien expresó su agradecimiento por la distinción conferida.

Además de sus certificados de participación en el Programa de Liderazgo, las graduandas de la Clase 2011 recibieron "citacions" de la oficina del gobernador Lincoln Chafee, la Vice gobernadora Elizabeth Roberts, los senadores Jack Reed y Sheldon Whitehouse, el congresista David Cicilline; la tesorera del Estado, Gina Raimondo, la representante Grace Díaz; así como de los alcaldes de Providence y Pawtucket, Ángel Taveras y Donald Grebien, respectivamente.

El LLI fue creado en **2003**, por iniciativa del RI Latino Civic Fund, con el objetivo de impulsar la formación de un liderazgo femenino emergente dentro de la comunidad. Líderes de los sectores público y privado reconocen la relevancia del programa de entrenamiento desarrollado por el Instituto.

El programa de formación se prolonga por cuatro meses con varias sesiones de trabajo en las que se entrena a las participantes en áreas de políticas públicas, superación personal, liderazgo, temas de salud que afectan a la mujer, voluntariado, manejo de estrategias, relaciones con los medios de comunicación, oratoria, defensoría, trabajo en equipo, asuntos de género, entre otras.

Las futuras líderes tienen la responsabilidad de conducir trabajos en equipo que resulten en proyectos de investigación en los que se identifican los problemas que afectan a la comunidad latina en Rhode Island, conjuntamente con recomendaciones y posibles soluciones para cada una de las áreas identificadas. Este año los proyectos versaron sobre temas de educación, salud y migración.

Forman parte también del Comité Coordinador del Programa de Líderes Latinas:

Doris Blanchard
Grace González
Osmary Rodríguez
Norelys Consuegra
Francia Pacheco
Vianela Núñez.

El RI Latino Civic Fund fue fundado en 2002 con la misión de promover la participación de la comunidad latina en la vida cívica y los procesos democráticos del estado de Rhode Island, a través de actividades como educación y registro para votantes, participación en procesos electorales y desarrollo de liderazgo.

Las graduandas entregaron una placa de reconocimiento al Comité Coordinador del Programa de Formación de Líderes Latinas. (Foto: Aníbal Melo)

Norelys Consuegra hace entrega del "Latina Leadership Award 2011" a la Concejal Sabina Matos. (Foto: Aníbal Melo)

2013 LLI

2014 LLI

New LLI Coordinator Norelys Consuegra
May 27, 2014

Queremos que conozcan a nuestra Coordinadora de Programa LLI Clase 2014 Norelys R. Consuegra Gracias Norelys por tu trabajo voluntario en LLI! — with Norelys Consuegra.

We want you to meet our new LLI Class 2014 Program Coordinator Norelys R. Consuegra Thank you Norelys for your volunteer work at LLI!

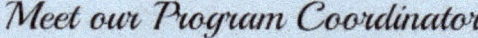
Meet our Program Coordinator

Norelys Consuegra has been working as a Senate Aide for U.S. Senator Jack Reed since 1996. Her duties include providing detailed information and assistance to the Senator's constituents in all areas of immigration law and policy among other issues pertaining to International Affairs.

Norelys graduated from the University of Rhode Island in 1996 with a degree in Political Science and Spanish and she completed her Masters degree in International Relations from Salve Regina University in 2012.

Thanks for being part of LLI. Your work inspire us!

Norelys R. Consuegra

RIPLA is proud to present the September Spotlight to the stronger woman and dedicated professional ever. Norelys has been tested in many ways with health challenges in her family and has always come out stronger giving us all a valuable lesson.

Norelys R. Consuegra, a native Rhode Islander, is Deputy Director of Elections for Rhode Island Secretary of State Nellie M. Gorbea. She received her undergraduate degree from the University of Rhode Island in 1996 and completed her master's degree in International Relations from Salve Regina University in 2012. Prior to her work in elections, she worked for U.S. Senator Jack Reed as a Senate Aide for 20 years.

Norelys is the recipient of the Ralph Gabellieri Service Award by Goodwill Industries of Rhode Island, has been recognized as a Diversity Ambassador by the State of Rhode Island, and was awarded the Extraordinary Women Award for community work. She's also received recognition from RI Latino Public Radio, the National Archives and Records Administration, and Telemundo Providence for her collaborative work in the community.

In addition to her full-time employment, she is an Adjunct Professor in the School of Continuing Studies at Roger Williams University. She has been involved in community service as a member of the Rhode Island Latino Civic Fund, Program Coordinator for the RI Latina Leadership Institute (LLI), and Secretary for the Pawtucket Youth Soccer Association. Most recently she has joined the boards of the Center for Civic Design and the Center for Technology & Civic Life, both non profit organizations that works toward promoting civic engagement. Norelys is a strong advocate for communities of color, the immigrant community, the LGBTQ community and enjoys teaching others about the importance of civic engagement. She makes her home in Johnston with her husband, Salvador, and three sons, Gabriel (19), Ashten (10) and her heart warrior, Tristen (2.5).

2014 -- H 8268

LC005812

S T A T E O F R H O D E I S L A N D
IN GENERAL ASSEMBLY
JANUARY SESSION, A.D. 2014

House Resolution Extending Congratulations

Introduced By: Representatives DeSimone, and Newberry Date Introduced: June 03, 2014 Referred To: House read and passed 1 WHEREAS, It has been made known to the House that certain persons and organizations 2 are deserving of commendation; and congratulating **Norelys Consuegra**; the outstanding achievement of your graduation from the 2014. 30. Rhode Island **New Leaders Council** Training Program

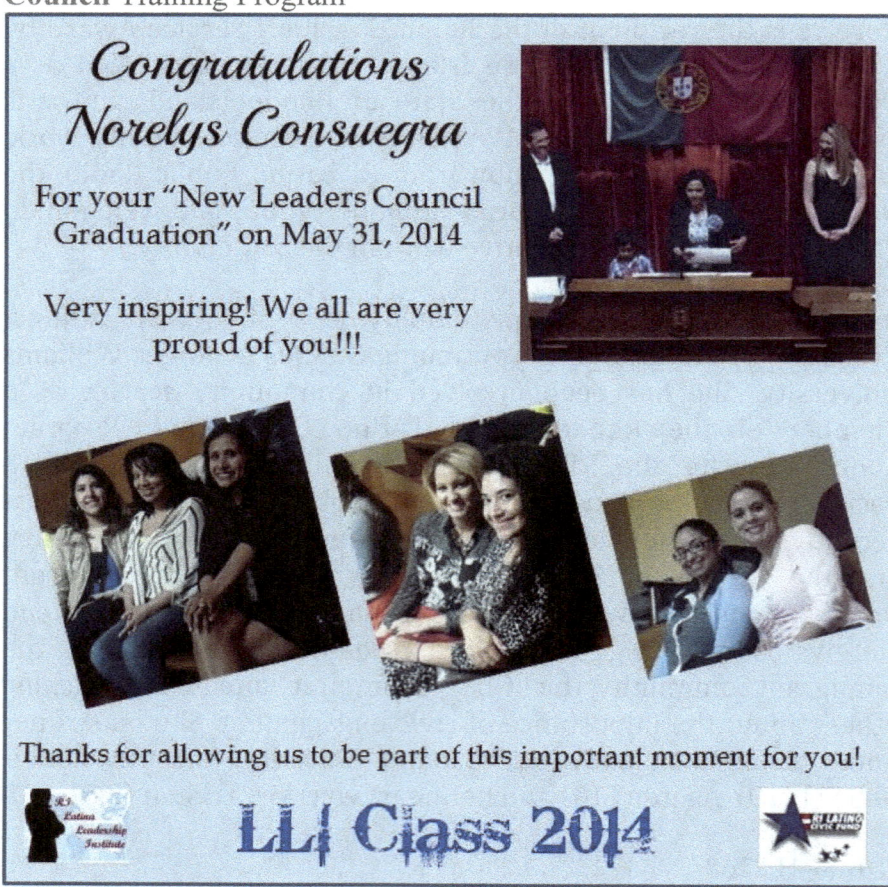

Great visit of the new President of RILCF to LLI, Jose Batista. Thank you!! **May 31, 2014**

Now in the annual membership meeting of RILCF and RILPAC, some of LLI class 2014 students and important community members and politics of RI. — with Taveras Lopez and 5 others. **June 11, 2014**

Dr. Domingo Morrel

Congratulations to Norelys R. Consuegra, Doris Blanchard, Sylvia Bernal and the 2014 Latina Leadership Institute (LLI) Graduates, President Jose F. Batista VP M Anyi Espinal for a successful class and gradation exercise. **November 15, 2014**

2015 LLI

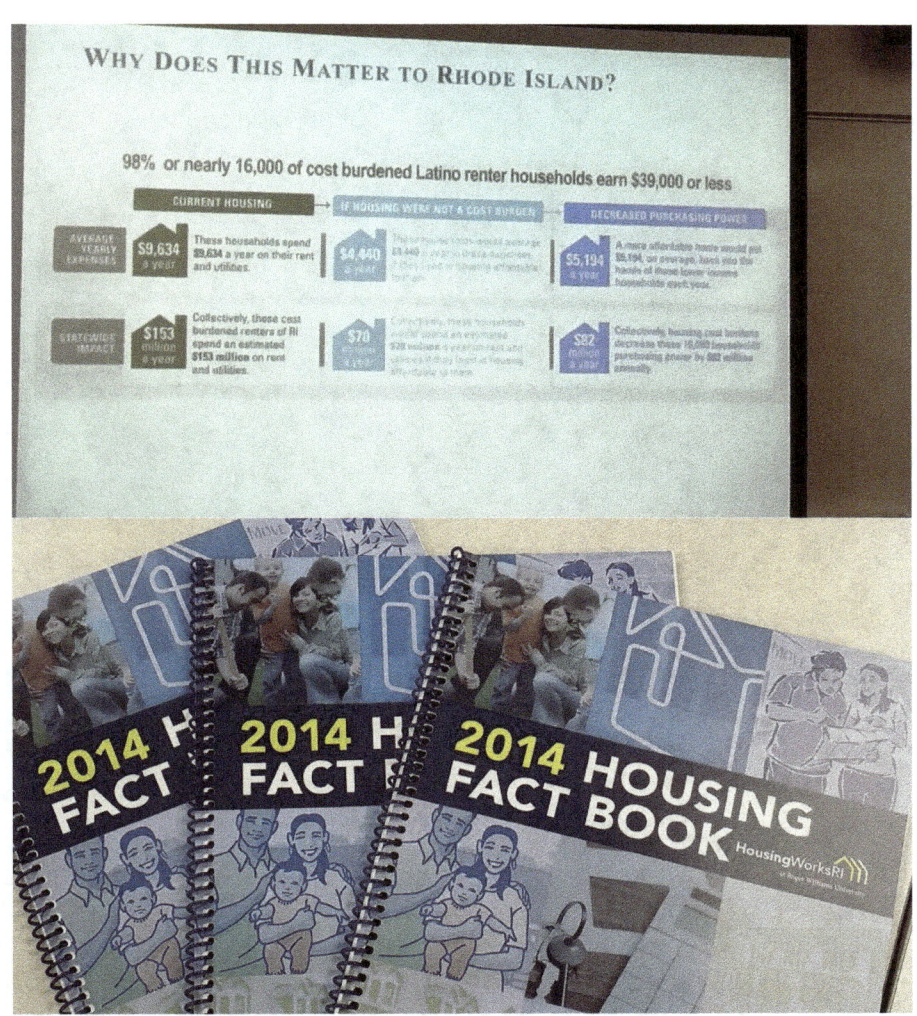

the Women's Fund
OF RHODE ISLAND

The mission of the Women's Fund of Rhode Island is to advance equity and social justice for women and girls. The Fund champions fairness, impartiality, opportunity, shared power and responsibility in all spheres of personal and community life including economic, cultural, educational, social, and political.

2016 LLI

A New Dawn for the Rhode Island Latina Leadership Institute (LLI)

Roger Williams University School of Continuing Studies partners with Rhode Island Latino Civic Fund

Tomás Ávila
July 14, 2016

Jose F. Batista, President of the Rhode Island Latino Civic Fund and Jamie Scurry, Dean Roger Williams University - School of Continuing Studies shake hands after signing Memorandum of Understanding between the two institutions.

In private ceremony July 14, 2016 Roger Williams University's School of Continuing Studies, signed a Memorandum Of Understanding (MOU) with the Rhode Island Latino Civic Fund (RILCF) to house the Latina Leadership Institute in its new Downtown Providence Campus at One Empire Place. a development that broadens the university reach into Providence's diverse local communities.

Norelys Consuegra, Coordinator of the Latina Leadership Institute and **Adjunct Professor in the School of Continuing Studies at Roger Williams University** started the dialogiue with Adriana Dawson, Assistant Dean, Admission and Community Engagement with community based organizations and traditionally underserved communities to extend academic and career development options to support their journey to self-sufficiency, during her employment interview. After many meetings and discussions, it concluded with official signing of the MOU, and the start of new Dawn for LLI.

Members of the Rhode Island Latino Civic Fund Andrea Bernal, Doris Blanchard, Norelys Consuegra, LLI Coordinator, Tomás Ávila, past Civic Fund President (220-2006), Betty Bernal Past Treasurer Civic Fund, Jose Batista, President RI Civic Fund ((2014-2017), Sylvia Bernal Past Treasurer RI Civic Fund Mr. Donald J. Farish (RIP), President Roger Williams University, Gonzalo Cuervo, Past President, RI Civic Fund during the July 14, 2016 RWU/RICF signing of Memorandum of Understanding.

Roger Williams' president Donald J. Farish, and Secretary of State Nellie Gorbea Chief of Staff Gonzalo Cuervo (Photo: Adriana Dawson)

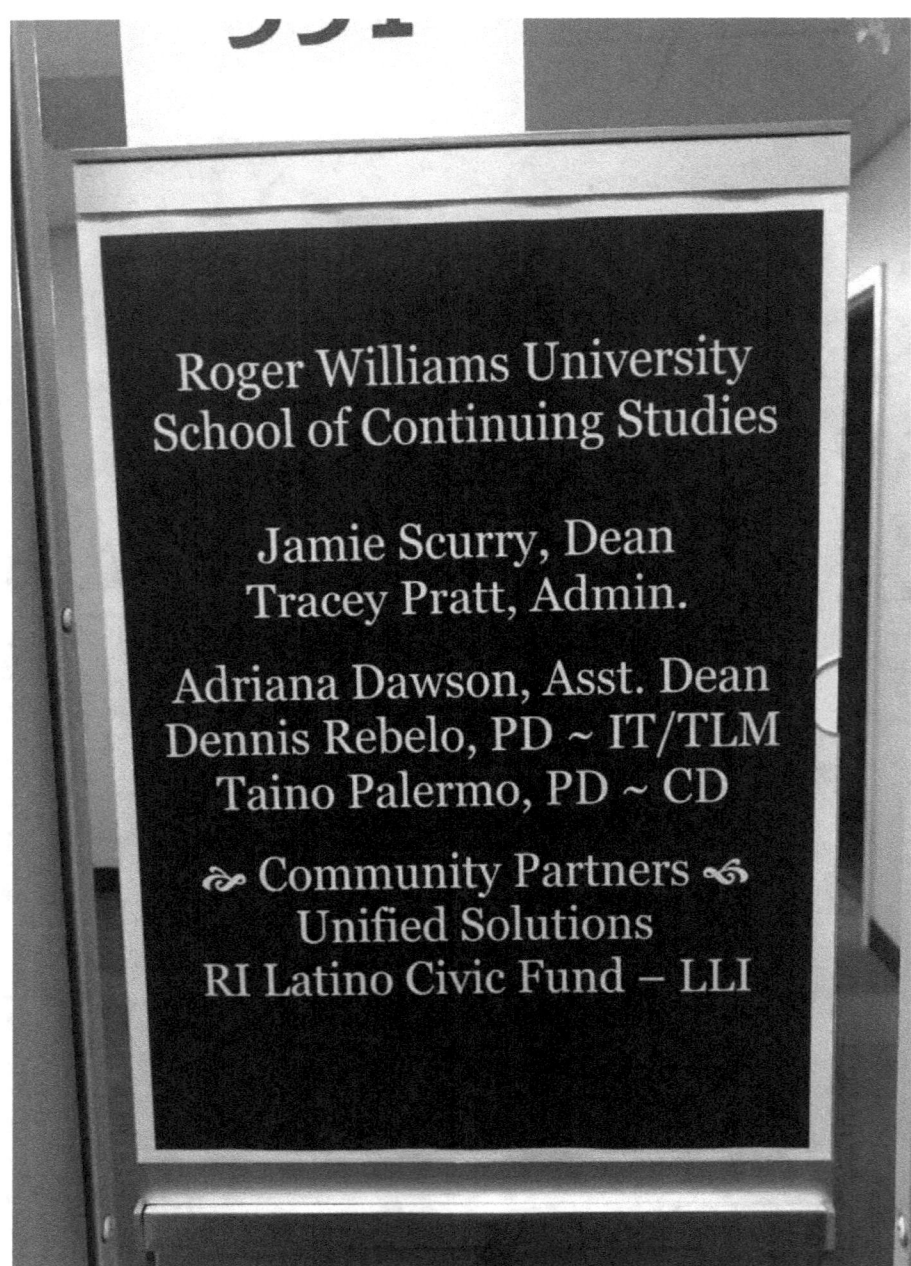

Comments

Norelys Consuegra, great vision to start the talks with Adriana Dawson on this partnership. Glad it became a reality RILCF has a home now, no more jumping around for LLI 😍 **Sylvia Bernal**

Great group effort, behind the scenes many conversations guided with the only purpose to apply our LLI mission "To empower Latinas in Rhode Island" 👏 👏 🙌 🙏 **Doris Blanchard**

So proud of the Leadership of Jose Batista and Adriana Dawson for make this possible. **Betty Bernal**

Congratulations to both RWU and RILCF for this new partnership!! So proud of everyone involved in making this happen!! **Delia Rodriguez Masjoan**

Felicidades, well done Mr. Batista. **Rep Grace Diaz**

Thank you Norelys Consuegra for your outstanding service as LLI Coordinator 2014-2019 and coordinating the LLI/RWU partnership along with Adriana Isaza Dawson in 2016, institutionalizing such a valuable platform for the future of Rhode Island. Welcome Melinda Lopez, newly appointed LLI Coordinator. Feliz 2020, Tomás Ávila, December 27, 2019

Adriana Dawson

Source: YW Magazine: SheShines, 2016
https://www.sheshines.org/2016-award-winners/adriana-dawson/#.XgXDoi9Omf0

Adriana Dawson serves as assistant dean of Professional Education & Employer Outreach for Roger Williams University's School of Continuing Studies in Providence. Prior, Dawson was the first female appointed state director for Rhode Island Small Business Development Center. During her 12-year tenure, Dawson led Rhode Island's first Latino Business Expo. Dawson is on the Board of Directors for United Way of Rhode Island, vice chair of Providence Economic Development Advisory Committee, member on Latino Policy Institute Advisory Board at Roger Williams University, and founding member of Girl Scouts of Southeastern New England's Hispanic Advisory Board. She was also appointed by Governor Raimondo to the Rhode Island Commission on Women. Dawson holds a Bachelor of Arts in Communication Studies from Northeastern University and a Master of Arts in Management & Organizational Communications from Emerson College.

At my core, I am a community agent. For as long as I can remember, my personal and professional journey has led me on a path to assist and advocate for those most vulnerable and whose voices are being silenced. Fortunately, for the past 17 years, my career has allowed me to help families and strengthen communities with a particular focus on economic empowerment and self-sufficiency.

I am now part of a team at Roger Williams University's School of Continuing Studies, led by Dean Jamie Scurry, which carries out this amazing work on a daily basis. We don't see ourselves just touching a student or program participant, we touch and transform families, neighborhoods, and communities. This work is done in collaboration with other community partners that share in the spirit of that mission.

In my current role overseeing the School of Continuing Studies Center for Workforce & Professional Development Career (CWPD), I support un/under employed individuals connect with our accelerated career pathway programs that prepares them for in demand industry opportunities and long term career success. There's Pivot the Hustle Program, where we and a cadre of dedicated volunteers support men and women within 18 months of release with self-discovery and soft skill job readiness training that will aid in their successful transition. We also work very closely with municipalities to help address their unique needs by developing customized programs for often times, their most vulnerable communities. This work is all carried out in a way that honors and values the individual, family, and culture.

Outside of my work environment, I've also committed to sitting on a number of boards and commissions that allow me to extend my efforts in this area. As a Commissioner on the Rhode Island Commission on Women and Girls, we're currently focused on addressing the wage inequity in Rhode Island. My role on the United Way of RI Board enables me to support an organization investing in programs and initiatives transforming communities, and my involvement with the Girls Scouts of Southeastern New England is helping them connect with a new and traditionally underserved membership demographic for GSSNE through their recently launched Hispanic Initiative.

In essence, helping families and lifting communities is in my DNA and I have the honor to assist people on a daily basis. I, myself, was a participant in many youth enrichment programs meant to assist teens from urban communities, particularly young women of color. I am also fortunate to come from a family of community servants and strong women! I now have a responsibility to do what I can to ensure that others have access, to help my daughter and other young girls of color feel like anything is possible, and that being bicultural/bilingual are assets not deficiencies.

My journey isn't over, in many ways, it's just beginning. There's a lot more work to be done and I'm ready!

Roger Williams University School of Continuing Studies partners with Rhode Island Latino Civic Fund

Posted Jul 14, 2016 at 12:53 PM
Updated Jul 14, 2016 at 3:56 PM

Roger Williams University deepens ties to Latino community

School of Continuing Studies dean Jamie E. Scurry, left, and Rhode Island Latino Civic Fund president Jose Batista. The Providence Journal/Steve Szydlowski.

PROVIDENCE — In a development that broadens its reach into diverse local communities, Roger Williams University's School of Continuing Studies on Thursday formally entered into a partnership with the Rhode Island Latino Civic Fund.

The latest in a series of community initiatives by Roger Williams, the new alliance is intended to provide greater education and workforce development opportunities for the state's substantial and increasing Hispanic population.

"The growth of the Latino community is even more noticeable and important in a community the size of Rhode Island, where Latinos are accounting for increasingly larger portions of the state population, local workforce and public schools," said Jose Batista, the fund's president. "As a result of this partnership, Latinos will have a broader network with which to share their talents and to learn new skills in order to build stronger communities."

Roger Williams' president Donald J. Farish said such community alliances reflect the philosophy that the school "is a private institution committed to serving the public good."

And in a multicultural world, Farish said, that means more than providing students merely a traditional model of higher education, one that begins after high-school graduation. He listed some of the more innovative opportunities that the new partnership — and existing ones with the cities of Central Falls and Pawtucket, and other community organizations — provide.

They include programs for "current high-school students interested in earning college credits while still in high school, working adults who want to acquire new knowledge to qualify for better jobs, recent parolees who need life skills to avoid going back to prison, and the economic needs of urban communities."

School of Continuing Studies dean Jamie E. Scurry, who has been instrumental in building the university's community partnerships, said that when she began her work in this area Roger Williams adhered to a longstanding model — one that was effective for some adults, but not necessarily for others.

"The School of Continuing Studies basically served what I would call your traditional adult learner," she said, "somebody who's already on a career pathway, already looking for a degree, and really needs a credential as much as they need to expand their knowledge. As well as active duty-military, a pretty traditional type of adult learning."

Scurry has led a four-year process of determining and meeting community needs — a process, she told The Providence Journal, that began with listening to individuals, community groups, municipalities and businesses.

The central question, she said, was how to develop programs for adults of any age, wherever they live, "no matter where they are on their journey, whether it's their second, third or fourth chance."

The new approach, she said, has transformed the School of Continuing Studies, which has associate's and bachelor's degree programs, along with certificate programs.

"It's a whole different way of thinking," Scurry said. "We can't sort of ride in on a white horse as an institution and say we have the answer. It's tearing down the walls and really saying, 'The community is like our campus. This is how we work together.' "

2017 LLI

On a cold winter night in the month of January, 10 Latinas met for the first time to begin a journey that would change their lives forever. These Latinas were skeptical at first but each willing to take a chance on learning more about their communities, learning more about their surroundings, about how they wanted to impact change, but most importantly, these Latinas took a chance on themselves.

The journey had its ups & downs, winter storms that caused havoc, a baby boy born that took away one of the elder Latina from this journey, the return of a former who provided much needed support and guidance, and other life commitments, yet in spite of these hurdles, the 10 Latinas did not give up and continued to grow as leaders and became an inspiration to many others.

Tonight, these powerful, dedicated, hardworking, totally awesome, Bad Ass Latinas proved that no matter the challenges, no matter the obstacles, they found themselves doing what they were born to do... To Inspire All Women to be their best, to run toward their dreams and make these dreams reality, no matter the hurdles.

Sue, Annette, Chris, Karen, Dorca, Glorisbel, Guisita, Joann, Janie and Stephanie, tonight you Inspired, You Lead, You Thrived. YOU ARE LLI. You came together and did an extraordinary job. So so proud and lucky to have met you. RI is better because of Leaders such as you.

Congratulations !

Norelys

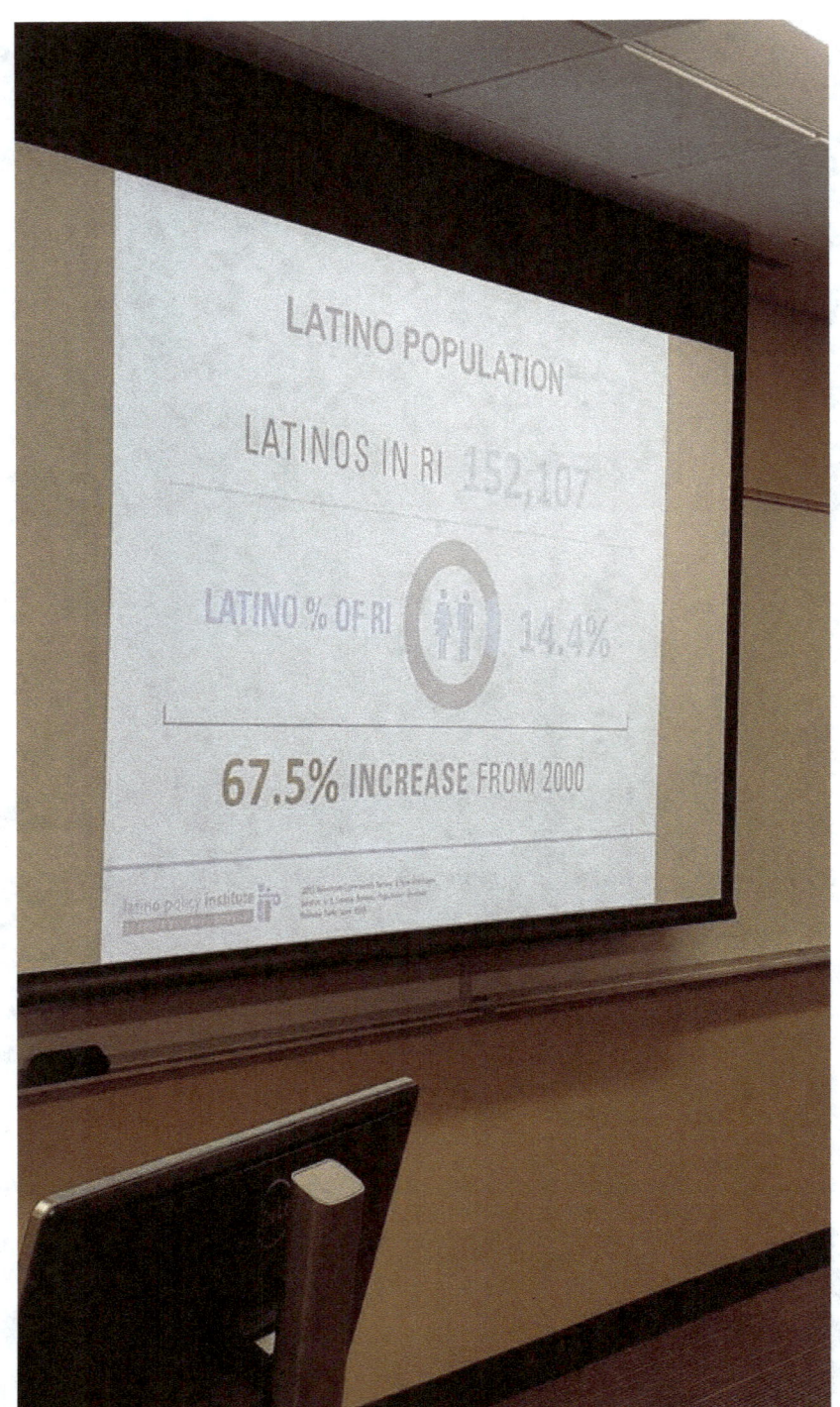

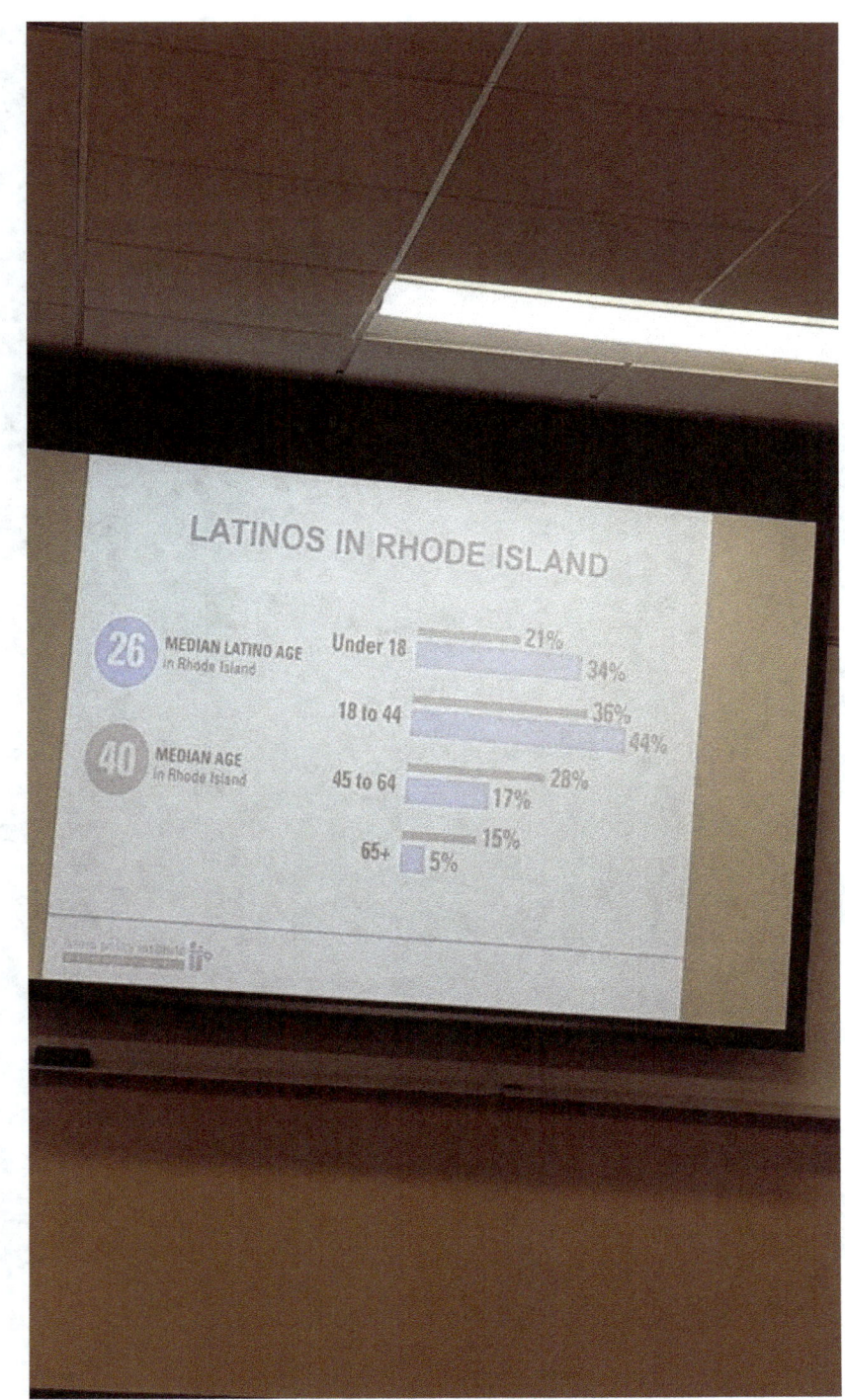

Arts for Education Fundraiser

ARTS for EDUCATION
FUNDRAISER

date   Thursday, June 15th 2017
time   5:30 PM - 7:30 PM
location   Hope Artiste Village - 1005 Main St., Pawtucket RI
tickets $20
contact   www.facebook.com/RILatinaLeadershipInstitute/

Latina Leadership Institute (LLI)

The mission of the Rhode Island Latina Leadership Institute (LLI) is to engage and encourage Latinas in Rhode Island to become community leaders through educational trainings and development with an emphasis in civic and community engagement.

LLI is a great opportunity for all Latinas who are seeking ways to connect with other community leaders to be an agent of change. Let LLI be part of your journey and take the first step to civic engagement.

Art for Education Fundraiser

The Latina Leadership class of 2017 has come together to host Arts for Education. This fundraiser will showcase local latin artists from our community, celebrate our latin culture and explore our similarities while supporting one another in the growth of learning through the arts. Proceeds will go towards scholarships for Latina women who are attending Roger Williams University for Continuing Studies in an effort to encourage their professional development.

In a world where people dance to the tune of others, the class of 2017 wants to empower women to have careers guided by the rhythm of endless possibilities. With your support they can make this a reality.

Help us reach our goal of raising $5,000

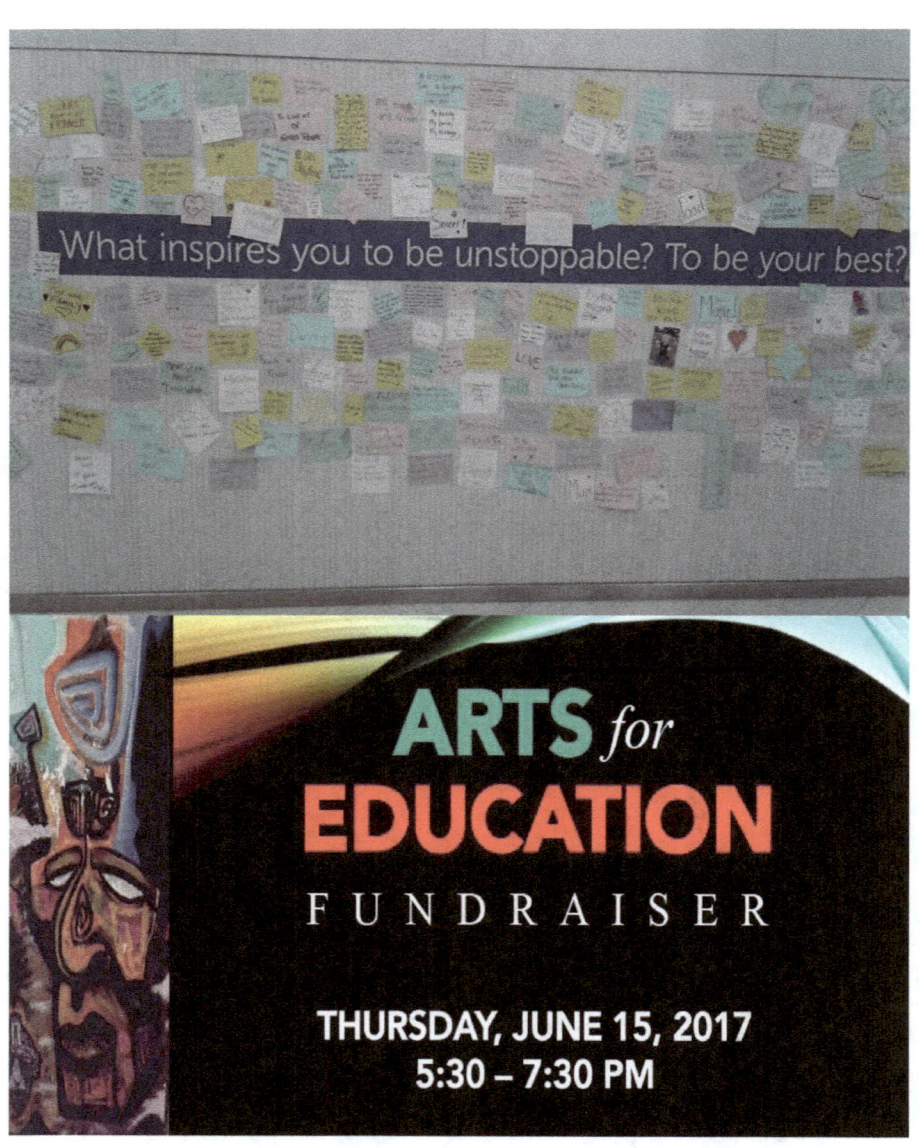

2018 LLI

February 26, 2019

We are so proud of you and so excited to see all the great work ahead. Thank you to Secretary of State Nellie M. Gorbea for hosting our reception and for being an Honorary LLI. To all the elected officials in attendance and their representatives, to all of our Alumni and of course, the members of the LLI Class 2018, family and friends. It has been an honor and privilege to have had the opportunity to be part of LLI and meet so many wonderful Latinas.

We have done some truly amazing things over the years and seeing the tremendous work many of our alumni are doing throughout Rhode Island affirms that LLI is the foundation of many Latina Leaders.
Thank you LLI for trusting us, for believing in yourselves and for taking that leap of faith. You are all inspirational, gifted and tremendas Lideres.

As Program Coordinators, it is our greatest challenge every year to make the next LLI better than the previous one. We cannot choose any one LLI class, as they are all are unique and special in their own way. Thank you to LLI 2018, for believing in our mission, vision and purpose.

Through the years, we have laughed, we have cried and we have learned so much from each other. Together we have accomplished so much.

You are hermanas, comadres, y confidentes. You embraced it and are now ready to get the work done. You have your carteritas of knowledge, use what you need, when you need, always looking for more stuff to put in.

We are so proud to have been part of your journey, a journey that began long before LLI. We just provided the tools to help you continue your personal journeys of success. You all have excelled and have reached some goals that you thought were impossible to reach and you have all succeeded. True leadership is not being the leader, but rather being a leader in many forms.

You are Latinas who are beautiful, bold, brave, caring, confident, courageous, dedicated, empowering, fearless, funny honest, inspiring and true leaders, YOU ARE LLI.

On behalf of the entire LLI staff, members of the RI Latino Civic Fund, Secretary of State Nellie Gorbea, thank you again.
Remember....

" Be careful of your thoughts, For your thoughts become your words;
Be careful of your words, For your words become your deeds;
Be careful of your deeds, For your deeds become your habits;
Be careful of your habits, For your habits become your character;
Be careful of your character, For your character becomes your destiny." Anonymous

Congratulations, YOU DID IT!

Thank Secretary of State Nellie M. Gorbea

Feb 20, 2019

LLI wishes to thank Secretary of State Nellie M. Gorbea for sponsoring the LLI Class 2018 Graduation Festivities. As a Latina and former RILCF President, we are honored to have her represent Rhode Island as a national figure and advocate, who is working to make sure all Rhode Islanders have access to the ballot box.

In addition, we want to congratulate this year's Alumni Award Recipients who will be honored during our graduation ceremony. This year we will be honoring 4 LLI Alumni who have taken the steps to pursue their goals, follow their dreams and be the voice of many who may not have the strength to do it themselves.

LLI brings together Latinas from all over Rhode Island, who seek to become engaged in our communities and offer safe spaces for other

Latinas to speak and seek their truth. We are so proud of the work all our alumni are doing; of getting involved and of finding their purpose.

Please join us in congratulating our LLI hermanas for being selected as

LLI Alumni Award Recipients:

Julia Gutierrez, LLI 13

for her courage to follow her passion and love of the Spanish Language and establishing "La Escuelita" so our children can continue to learn and speak our mother tongue.

Maria Rivera, LLI 14

for her desire to work for her community to provide opportunities for all Central Fall residents and for being a humanitarian champion for her Puerto Rican brothers and sisters.

Andrea Gomez, LLI 15

or her passion to speak up for those who cannot, to teach us about diversity and inclusion and to remind us all that we are all human, no matter our multiple identities.

Dorca Paulino, LLI 17

for breaking through the barrier and becoming the face of equity in our State's Judiciary branch and showing our youth of color that they too can be lawyers and judges.

This is LLI, you are LLI and it has been our honor and pleasure to be part of your journey.

CONGRATULATIONS TO OUR GRADUATES AND AWARD RECEPIENTS. #LLI2018

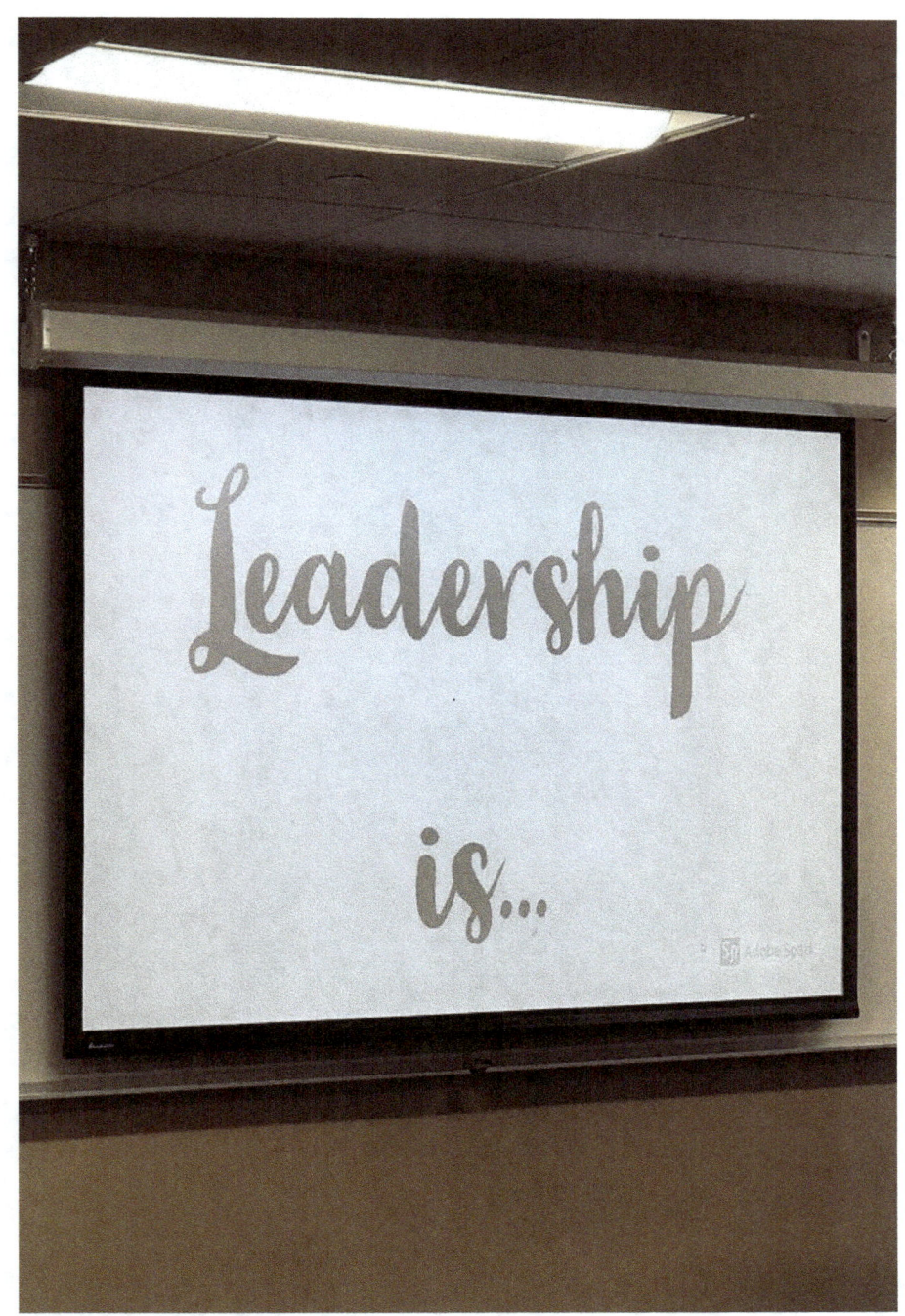

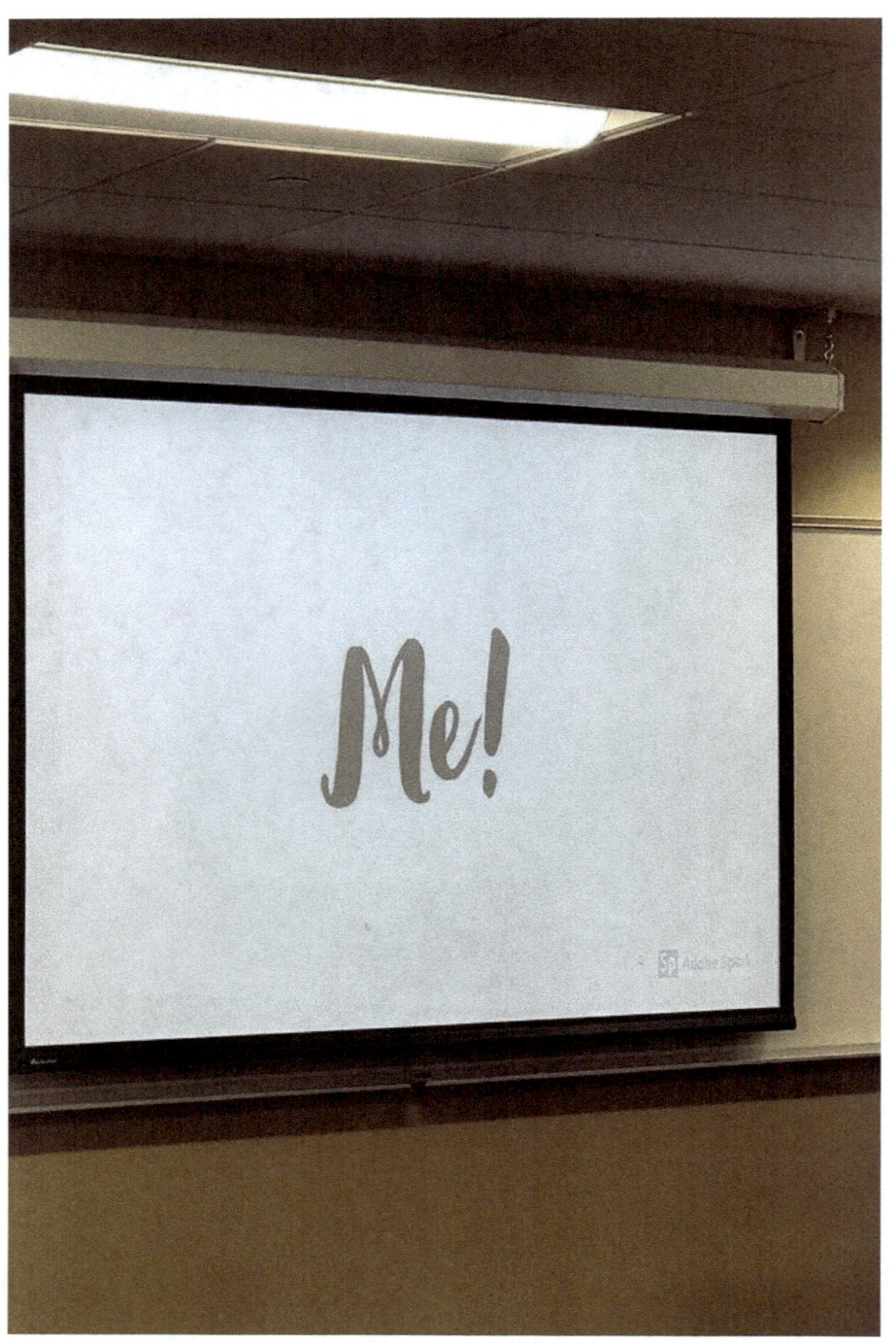

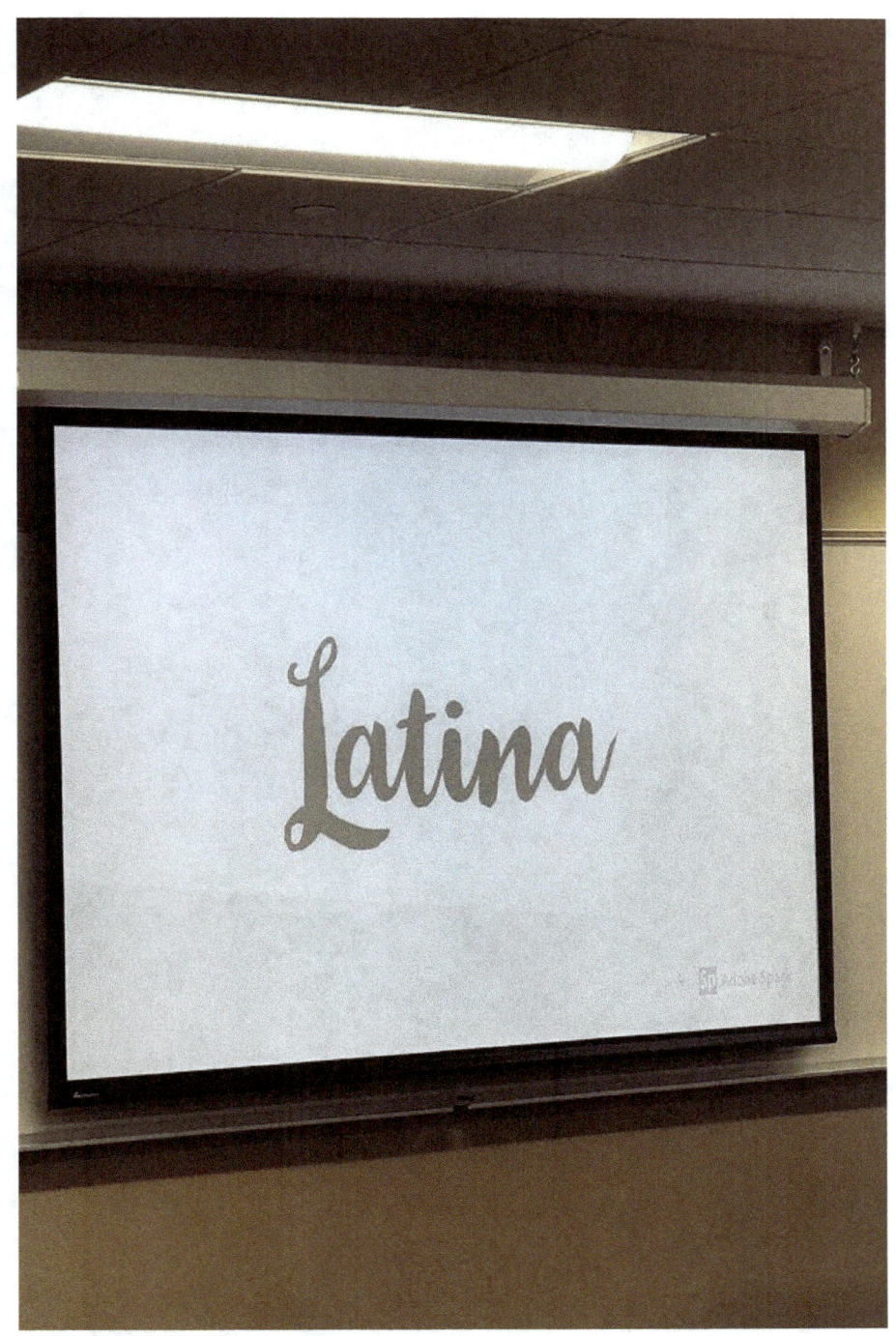

16th Annual National Association of Student Personnel Administrators
New England Latinx Student Leadership Conference

CLAIM YOUR DREAMS EMBRACE YOUR FUTURE

Friday-Saturday, April 5-6

Free to Rhode Island College Students

Celebrate the cultural diversity of the Latinx community, examine issues pertinent to Latinx students, communities and culture, and foster connections among Latinx college students within the region.

Featured Speakers

Samantha Ramirez-Herrera
Entrepreneur, Filmmaker and
Civil Rights Activist

Sarita Brown
President of Excelencia
in Education

ric.edu/latinx

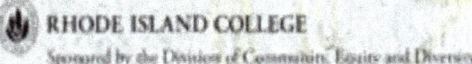
RHODE ISLAND COLLEGE
Sponsored by the Division of Community, Equity and Diversity

NASPA
Student Affairs Administrators
in Higher Education

Latina Leadership Institute

CONGRATULATIONS RI LATINA LEADERSHIP INSTITUTE CLASS OF 2018

Ava Moreno, Melinda Lopez, Veronica Castaneda, Leonor Tavarez, Elizabeth Hernandez, Gabriela Ledesma, Karla Liza Minelly, Tatiana Baena, Amanda Ruiz, Catherine Hidalgo, Michelle Freitas and Tatiana Valencia.

RI Latina Leadership Institute Class 2018

Graduation Ceremony

**February 25, 2019
RI State House**

12 Graduate from Latina Leadership Institute

Tuesday, February 26, 2019
GoLocalProv News Team

Rhode Island Latino PAC and the RI Latino Civic Fund is celebrating the graduation of 12 participants from the Latina Leadership Institute (LLI).

The graduation marks the 13th group of students that have completed the program, and the 15th year the Civic Fund has provided this signature program.

"LLI has been a cornerstone of the Rhode Island Latino Civic Fund's programming since its inception. The Latino community in Rhode Island is at its strongest when each and every member feels empowered and engaged in their local community. LLI has filled a very specific need that has continued to develop the leaders of future. I congratulate each and every graduate of the 2018 cohort," said RILCF Vice President Marcela Betancur.

Each graduate joins the Latina Leadership Alumni Association upon graduation.

The Institute

The Institute provides Latinas interested in civic engagement with the opportunity to forge relationships and networks with local community members while exploring various fields of interest.

"These women excel in their personal spaces and are ready to add to the numerous LLI alumni that call Rhode Island home. They are ready to take the lessons they have learned from the program and apply it back to their communities and to our state in order to make a more prosperous Rhode Island for all," said Norelys Consuegra, one of LLI's program coordinators.

It combines leadership training and development with practical experience in local civic engagement over ten sessions.

The Graduates are Listed Below

Certificates of Graduation

Tatiana Baena	Aura A. Moreno
Veronica Castaneda	Elizabeth Munoz
Michelle P Freites	Karla Minelly-Roper
Catherine I Hidalgo	Amanda M Ruiz
Gabriela Ledesma	Leonor M Tavarez
Melinda López	

Certificate of Participation

Tatiana Valencia

LLI has Gone International

Maria Rivera
Central Falls City Council President
July 19, 2019

Congratulations to Fiorella Cipriani, LLI 14 on achieving your goal in Lima, Peru and Maria Rivera LLI14 for your support.

Quien iba a decir que 5 años después de LLI estaría en Peru dando una conferencia sobre el empoderamiento a la mujer con mi hermana de LLI y Presidenta de Comunde - Corporación Mundial de Empresarios Fiorella. Te felicito por tu 1er Congreso Mundial de empresarios.

Bendecida por las oportunidades que se me siguen brindando pero sobre todo feliz de poder hablar sobre un tema tan delicado que no es fácil de asimilar por muchos en otros países, que es la igualdad a la mujer.

How to express my sincere appreciation

Norelys Consuegra
February 27, 2019

How to express my sincere appreciation to so many people that have supported me through my time with LLI. Last night was my last graduating class and I am still in awe of the love that has grown with all of my LLI sisters.
The decision to step down as Coordinator was not easy, but as with all decisions, we pray and hope that it is the right one. I know that LLI will be in good hands and that the next Coordinator will fall in love with her just like I did in 2006. She has been part of me for so long and I know that because of her, I have had the strength to face many challenges in my life. She gave me the strength and courage to leave my job of 20 years in pursue of a new and exciting career in elections, and now she has given me the unconditional love of my alumni, who understand why I must move on to other adventures.

I thank my husband Salvador Sarmiento, who has been by my side since I began my LLI journey, my children who spent many Saturdays without mommy and my family for always supporting my events.

To my faculty, who always said yes to facilitating a session, free of charge and giving their best to a group of eager learners. I am truly blessed to be able to count of so many people.

To Doris Blanchard, for taking this walk with me and celebrating my ideas. Thank you for trusting me.

To all LLI alumni for allowing me share my knowledge, embracing my ideas and for the love of our sisterhood. You I will miss the most.

It has truly been an honor. Thank you.
 Nore

The Rhode Island Latino Civic Fund seeks two volunteer Co-Directors for the Latina Leadership Institute (LLI). LLI's mission is to engage and foster Rhode Island Latinas to become community leaders through educational trainings and development with an emphasis in civic and political engagement.

Reporting to the Board of Directors, the Co-Directors are responsible for:
- Developing and delivering an annual leadership training program that includes, but is not limited to:
    - Civic and community engagement
    - Personal and professional development
    - Fundraising practices
    - Other relevant topics such as: campaign management, policy, etc.
- Inviting community leaders to sessions and providing networking opportunities for participants
- Recruiting 10-20 Latinas to participate in the program each session
- Engaging LLI alumni and building a network to support participants and programming
- Maintain clear records of financial expenditures and revenues for the Board of Directors with help from the Board's Treasurer
- Provide regular updates on activities and seek input from the Board of Directors

Each co-director will serve a minimum of two years.

In your cover letter, please address the following questions:

- Are you a graduate of LLI? If so, what year did you graduate?
- What makes you the best fit as the co-director of LLI?
- If given the opportunity, what programmatic or structural changes would you make to LLI?
- What is your vision for LLI in five years?

Interested candidates should submit a resume and cover letter to:

rilatinaleadershipinstitute@gmail.com *by September 1, 2019*

Melinda Lopez Appointed Director

October 7, 2019

We are proud to announce today that Melinda Lopez will serve as the new Director of the Latina Leadership Institute (LLI), a cornerstone program that teaches Latinas from all across the state skills in advocacy, community organizing, fundraising, and communications with the aim of promoting positive change in Rhode Island.

The RI Latino Civic Fund and the RI Latina Leadership Institute is excited to welcome Lopez, a LLI 2018 alumna, into her new role as the organization aims to launch another class in the fall of 2020.

Melinda López was born and raised in New York City. She received her B.A. in Psychology from Brown University and her Teacher Certification from Roger Williams University. She has been an educator since 1994, working in both early childhood, elementary and higher education settings. For over 10 years Melinda has been designing and facilitating professional development for adults. Melinda is an Adjunct Professor at Rhode Island College and a Latina Leadership Institute graduate.

In 2019 she also completed national training in Washington, DC from Emerge America. Melinda seeks to become the first Puerto Rican to serve in Rhode Island's General Assembly. Melinda's 2020 campaign will focus on engaging and elevating the Johnston community within Rhode Island politics. She lives with her partner Francisco, her sons Joseph (13) and Jaxon (20), and their dog Jake.

Norelys R. Consuegra

RIPLA is proud to present the September Spotlight to the stronger woman and dedicated professional ever. Norelys has been tested in many ways with health challenges in her family and has always come out stronger giving us all a valuable lesson.

Norelys R. Consuegra, a native Rhode Islander, is Deputy Director of Elections for Rhode Island Secretary of State Nellie M. Gorbea. She received her undergraduate degree from the University of Rhode Island in 1996 and completed her master's degree in International Relations from Salve Regina University in 2012. Prior to her work in elections, she worked for U.S. Senator Jack Reed as a Senate Aide for 20 years.

Norelys is the recipient of the Ralph Gabellieri Service Award by Goodwill Industries of Rhode Island, has been recognized as a Diversity Ambassador by the State of Rhode Island, and was awarded the Extraordinary Women Award for community work. She's also received recognition from RI Latino Public Radio, the National Archives and Records Administration, and Telemundo Providence for her collaborative work in the community.

In addition to her full-time employment, she is an Adjunct Professor in the School of Continuing Studies at Roger Williams University. She has been involved in community service as a member of the Rhode Island Latino Civic Fund, Program Coordinator for the RI Latina Leadership Institute (LLI), and Secretary for the Pawtucket Youth Soccer Association. Most recently she has joined the boards of the Center for Civic Design and the Center for Technology & Civic Life, both non profit organizations that works toward promoting civic engagement. Norelys is a strong advocate for communities of color, the immigrant community, the LGBTQ community and enjoys teaching others about the importance of civic engagement. She makes her home in Johnston with her husband, Salvador, and three sons, Gabriel (19), Ashten (10) and her heart warrior, Tristen (2.5).

Alumni

Sabina Matos

Councilwoman of Ward 15 Olneyville, Valley, Silver Lake and West End Districts At the age of 20, Sabina Matos '01 left the Dominican Republic for America. Her father was mayor of Paraiso, a small town in the Province of Barahona; her mother, a teacher. One of six children, Matos remembered that their home was always open to the community, to anyone in need. "If someone needed to go to the hospital and didn't have the resources, they came to my father.

If someone died and their family didn't have resources, the family came to our house. After we moved from Paraiso to the capital, people from our hometown who had errands in the capital would stay at our house," she said. Matos said she learned about public service simply by observing her mother and father. In America, Matos transferred from CCRI to RIC as an ESL student. "The ESL professors were inspiring," she said. "They made you feel that you could do anything. I chose a major in communication." She laughs, thinking about it now. "I ask myself how I could dare to choose a communication major when I was too shy and didn't speak English well."

Upon graduating from RIC in 2001, Matos was not yet a citizen of the U.S., yet she would become a great advocate of the U.S. Constitution. She helped organize the 2003 Immigrant Workers Freedom Ride, where thousands of immigrants, union members and elected officials rallied in New York and Washington, D.C., in support of immigrant and workers' rights. As an employee of the nonprofit group Making Connections Providence, she helped residents of Elmwood, South Providence and West End neighborhoods improve jobs, education and housing in their communities. In 2005 she was finally able to change her "legal resident" status to "U.S. citizen." The following year she voted for the first time, with her name on the ballot. It was her first, though unsuccessful, run for city council. In 2010 Matos won the council seat. She said she intends to help the underserved in her community. "A young man wrote asking me for help," she said. "He wanted to go to Classical High School, but the waiting list is extremely long.

Considering all the challenges around him, the challenges of the neighborhood he lives in, it was very satisfying to see how good his grades were. It made me want to do more. I'm in a position to help people like him." Matos said there needs to be more schools like Classical and more options for students seeking quality education. Quality education, she said, should not be a privilege. Matos said her one regret as a RIC alum is not getting more involved in student organizations. "I was too shy, too new to the country. I encourage students to get involved in organizations at RIC and also to find out what is happening in their neighborhoods. There are many neighborhood projects that need volunteers." Matos is on the board of the United Way of Rhode Island and a past board member of the Olneyville Housing Corporation and the Olneyville Neighborhood Association. She is a past president of the Rhode Island Latino Civic Fund, the Latina Leadership Institute and the R.I. Latino Political Action Committee. Currently she is associate director of New Roots Providence, which offers free training, grants and technical assistance to nonprofit organizations throughout Rhode Island. By all accounts, it appears that the shy communication major

9 things to know about R.I. Sen.-elect Sandra Cano's politics, policies

By G. Wayne Miller
Journal Staff Writer

Posted Apr 8, 2018 at 11:23 AM
Updated Apr 9, 2018 at 8:57 AM

The newly elected senator from Pawtucket sits down with The Journal to go over her stances on many issues, from education and rebuilding Rhode Island's crumbling schools to keeping the Pawtucket Red Sox in the city.

Pawtucket Democrat Sandra Cano last week was overwhelmingly voted into the state Senate in a special election. An at-large city councilwoman, Cano, 34, is the assistant vice president of business and community development at Navigant Credit Union. Born and raised in Medellin, Colombia, Cano immigrated to the U.S. at the age of 16. She joins the General Assembly with a robust agenda for her District 8 and Rhode Island as a whole.

Meeting with The Providence Journal on Sunday, Cano talked about some of her priorities:

1. Schooling

"Education is the key to success. I have proven that myself. Throughout my career it has been education that has been the component of my life that has helped me develop and bring a different perspective to the table." Cano attended the Community College of Rhode Island, and holds a bachelor's degree from Bryant University and a master's from the University of Rhode Island. A Spanish-speaker only until 16, she learned English in Rhode Island schools.

2. Rebuilding Rhode Island's crumbling schools

"An environment for the children to learn, for them to be able to feel comfortable, is extremely important. We have to do more, which is why I am extremely supportive of the $250 million for schools to continue to be fixed." The senator-elect supports Gov. Gina Raimondo's proposed $250-million bond to accomplish the first stage of a statewide repair program.

3. Empowering women

"It is very important that women are heard, that we have a voice at the table. We have some rights that have been taken away, and that I think are still not taken too seriously, like it should be. Right now, it is important to have that voice at the table, to continue to advocate, and I'm here to do so for those that don't have a voice."

4. Keep the PawSox in Pawtucket?

Most definitely. "They have been an icon of our city. They are part of the fabric of our city, as well. And I do believe that they are a great community partner. Their investment in our city, in downtown Pawtucket, is going to be a catalyst for other businesses to come and to stay."

5. Keeping Hasbro world headquarters in Pawtucket

"Economic development is extremely important, to support small businesses and to make sure that Pawtucket is a destination and we have good-quality jobs in our city. Keeping Hasbro in our city as one of the manufacturing companies that we do have, and as a worldwide-known company, is certainly a priority for me."

6. Deferred Action for Childhood Arrivals, or DACA "Dreamers"

"That's part of my DNA. I'm an immigrant. I came here at the age of 16 under political asylum, so I do believe that these students have a lot of potential and need to have the support to continue their education. Those are our future doctors, our future CEOs — and even a senator!"

7. Opioid users and people with mental-health needs

"It is a big population that needs support." Cano backs legislation championed by state Sen. Joshua Miller and others to address these crises.

8. The arts

"We do have amazing artists in our city and we need to continue supporting them as entrepreneurs, as the good group that make our city really innovative." Cano recognizes the importance of the arts to all of Rhode Island, but said, with a laugh, "selfishly I do like to have Pawtucket in the front row of the arts in Rhode Island."

9. Expanding solar and wind power

"We could have a lot of savings and we could be ahead of the game when it comes to renewable energy projects. It's a very important thing we could do across the state."

Read Cano's stands on all of her issues at sandracano.weebly.com/issues.html

— gwmiller@providencejournal.com

(401) 277-7380

On Twitter: @GWayneMiller

My Journey To Launching My Nonprofit CaneiWalk

by Stephanie Olarte
04/1/19|

Our LLI Alumni continue to shine, Stephanie Olarte Arango, **LLI 2017**, you are amazing. Nothing can stop you. Congratulations.

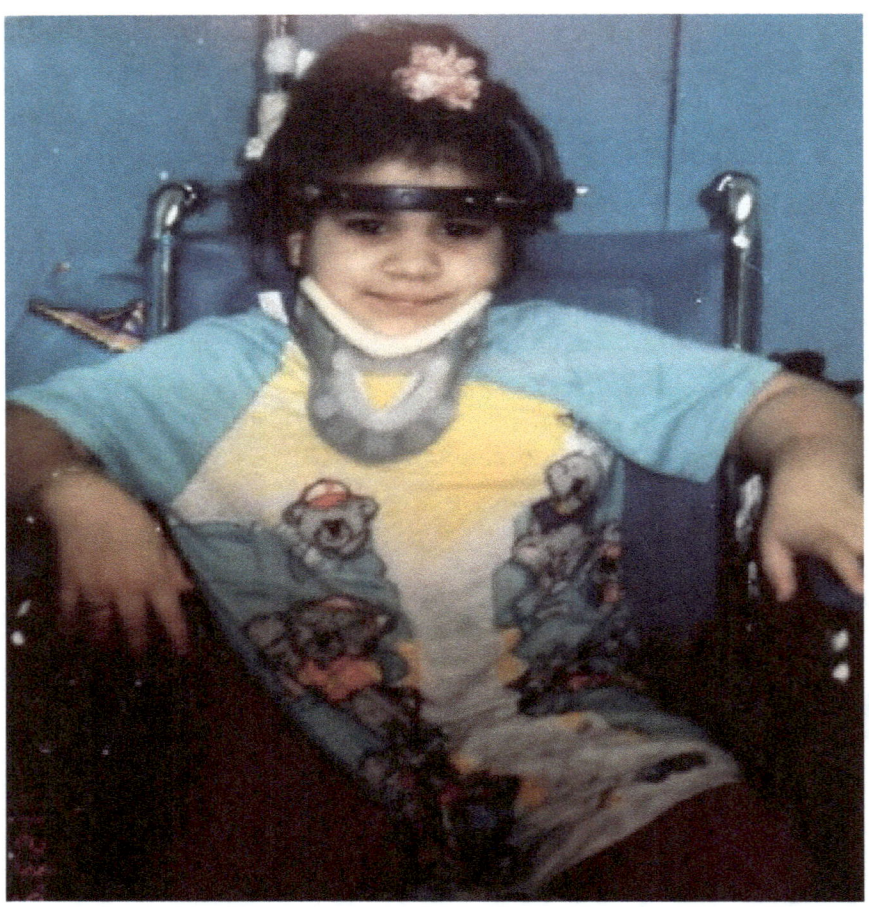

As a child I didn't have an organization or program that told me it was okay to be disabled. That I was still strong. That I was capable of achieving anything I wanted. I had to learn that on my own with a lot of heartbreak.

I was born with a severe and rare version of scoliosis that didn't really develop until I was about 7 years old. I was a fun energetic kid! As I grew, my disability got worse, I became weak and less active. I had a series of surgery and treatments and my childhood was flipped and I matured rather quickly. Fortunately, I had a loving and hard-working mother who was supportive and wanted me to know that I was no different than anyone else, but at the time I felt that a mother had to say those things, so I did not really give her credit. I didn't feel that I was like anyone else anymore. I went from a playful child that ran around with her friends, to being in a wheelchair unable to move or walk. I knew I was different and at the time I didn't like it!

I was homeschooled for a year during my third grade which was when I had my first major surgery and when I returned to school my friends didn't treat me the same. People were at first walking on eggshells with me, and eventually that turned into a lot of bullying and misunderstanding that left me feeling less than my peers. I had to learn to overcome these struggles alone because there really weren't any programs that dealt with disabled students and helped us feel included in day-to-day activities. Disabled youth didn't have the luxury of having an organization specifically for them that build their confidence and empowered them academically as well as emotionally.

I had so many unhealthy experiences that I had to go through in school and outside of school that really shaped who I am today. One of the big turning points for me was when I was told that college was going to be so difficult and I should forget about applying as my disability would not allow me to succeed, nor achieve a degree. At this point in my life I had a problem with authority and when my high school counselor said those words to me my first reaction was to cry, and my second reaction was to apply to college because how dare she underestimate my value and motivation to succeed. Of course, I didn't listen to her. I went to college and I have two degrees and I now work hard as a professional and as an advocate for people in my community.

About three years ago I was looking for jobs and nothing was happening - no calls, no interviews, nothing! I had the worse luck! All those negative thoughts that I had as a child creeped back up and I kept questioning myself. Am I worth it? Am I capable? Is this disability keeping me from succeeding?! However, one day I realized that these thoughts were not okay. I think about it now and I feel ashamed that I was doubting myself. I was worth it then and worth it now. I am capable and my disability is an asset. I tell myself this every day and it is still something I am working on believing. When I came to this realization a bigger picture came to mind. I had to do something that will teach people that disability is not a liability. I wanted to target the youth and let them know that no matter their condition they are an asset! That was how I first thought about the development of CaneiWalk.

Is there anything in RI that will help disabled youth? NO! Since I was a child, to my surprise, nothing had changed and these programs still weren't available. Sure, we had TRIO program (I participated on those as well) but they don't focus so much on specific needs of certain students, particularly disabled students. So, I decided to be the change agent!

CaneiWalk has been a project that I have been working on for about three years. What helped me take the lead was New Leaders Council RI, giving me tools that I would need to bring the project to life. This past month, we finally became a 501c3 a nonprofit organization that works to empower and amplify the voices of youth with disabilities to reach their full potential by providing innovative mentoring, youth leadership development and social justice/civic and community engagement programs. We want to motivate our disabled youth to reach their personal, educational and professional goals while guiding our public and private sectors to be more inclusive.

It certainly has not been an easy task, especially being the only organization of its kind in Rhode Island. Fundraising, and getting

community members excited has been challenging. However, having persisted my entire life to succeed for my family and myself, now I will do it for our disabled youth, because they deserve a better future!
Feel free to check out our website, www.caneiwalk.org! your support is imperative for our success!

Stephanie Olarte is the Rhode Island State Program Coordinator for The Hispanic Federation and the founder of CaneiWalk. She is a Latina and disability advocate, and is passionate about seeing more women of color elected to office.

Sign-up here for updates from The BGG so you don't miss the latest posts! Don't forget to follow us on Facebook, Twitter, and Instagram too!

Soljane Martinez

Ed.D candidate, Consultant, Educator, Mom

The education field demands daily, often hour-to-hour flexibility in an effort to serve all students holistically. I'm a driven and positive professional whose first priority is always the interests of my clients; providing capability, adaptability, and scalability.

With more than 20 years of experience in both media and education, I know what it takes to engage all stakeholders when it comes to decisions regarding the equitable education of ALL students.

My experience as an educator includes:

Classroom teacher of grades 3-12 in New York City and Rhode Island
History Department Chair
Regional educational representative of Civics Education
Social & Restorative Justice education
Dean of Culture & Students
Principal
Lifelong learner!

I hold a BA in Journalism from the University of Rhode Island ('98); Masters in Education from CUNY-Staten Island ('03) and expect to receive my Educational Leadership Doctoral degree from Johnson & Wales University in 2020.

In addition to loving all things education, I am the proud mother of two boys--middle school and high school-aged. I fill my days with fun by dancing while cooking alongside my loving husband.

Throughout the years, I've participated in a variety of on-going professional development opportunities as well as taken leadership roles in educational organizations.

In 2008 I was chosen as a Freedom Writer Teacher, learning from Erin Gruwell, how to implement the Freedom Writers Methodology, a progressive teaching philosophy with curricula designed to achieve excellence from all students.
In 2013, I was appointed to the iCivics Educator Network by (retired) Supreme Court Justice Sandra Day O'Connor. My then 8th grade students and I had the pleasure of hosting her in our classroom that same year to display our unrelenting commitment to civic education and social justice.

In 2014, I was chosen as one of 24 educators worldwide, to be a part of the USC Shoah Foundation and Discovery Education's The Past is Present. I joined other educators, students and Holocaust survivors for a week in Poland to commemorate the 70th anniversary of the liberation of the Auschwitz concentration camp.

In 2017, I was featured in Edutopia's Schools That Work series for my diversity work with students including my work with English language learners.

Roger Williams University deepens ties to Latino community

Tatiana Baena

Central Falls City Council At Large

Tatiana Baena·Tuesday, December 3, 2019

Tatiana was born in Medellin, Colombia, and migrated with her family to the United States, arriving in Central Falls, Rhode Island. Almost 20 years later, Tatiana still resides in Central Falls, on the same street where she grew up.

Tatiana has been serving as the Director of Enrichment Opportunities at the Central Falls School District for over a year, working to cultivate community partnerships and secure out-of-school time programs for our students. For the past five years, she has stayed active in the city by combining her love of soccer and community to organize the Mundialito Soccer Tournament, which she founded to raise funds to provide non-traditional scholarships to Central Falls student-athletes.

Tatiana is a member of the Central Falls Alumni Association and the City Planning Board, serving as Vice-Chair for the past two years. She also serves as the Treasurer of the Colombian American Cultural Society Board of Directors and was recently elected Vice-Chair of the Central Falls Prevention Coalition for substance abuse awareness and prevention.

A 2008 graduate of Central Falls High School, Tatiana went on to earn a Bachelor of Business Administration from the University of Rhode Island in 2012. She belongs to several leadership groups focused on developing and supporting future leaders, including New Leaders Council of RI, Latina Leadership Institute of RI, and Millennial RI.

Tatiana is a true Warrior and is looking forward to creating more opportunities for Central Falls' youth to learn and be engaged, leveraging more resources for our community, and empowering our people. Tatiana may be reached at teambaena@gmail.com or 401-365-0864.

Campaign Announcement

After an amazing Thanksgiving holiday spent with family and friends and reflecting on the people and things that are important to me, I realize that I want to contribute more to the community that has given me so much. I want to create more opportunities for our youth to learn and be engaged and leverage more resources for our community. I want to create and strengthen programs and policies that empower our people. I want to continue to be a strong voice in Central Falls and bring my current efforts, which many of you have generously supported, to the next level.

That's why I invite you to join me on Tuesday, December 17th, at 6:00 pm at Taqueria Lupita to kickoff my campaign for City Council At Large in Central Falls.

That day, I will also be collecting basic necessities for Central Falls families in need. Items including winter gear, cleaning supplies, and personal hygiene products would be greatly appreciated. In the meantime, LIKE my new page Tatiana Baena, to follow my journey! Hope to see you all on the 17th!

#FromTheCommunity #ForTheCommunity

Obed Papp

President RIPLA
LLI2009

Obed is the President of the Rhode Island Professional Latino Association (RIPLA), she currently serves as the Director of the Drug Free Community program in the Healthy Community office of the City of Providence.

Mrs. Papp has her Bachelors degree in Economics and received a Specialist degree in Public Government Adminsitration a certificate in Prevention Specialist and a Masters in Public Administration from University of Rhode Island and. She is of Colombian descent and speaks fluent Spanish offering a multi-cultural perspective in the community of Rhode Island

Obed has been very active in the greater Providence community serving as an ambassador of good will. For ten years, Obed has been committed to working on two important areas in public service and these areas are community development and politics. Obed received in 2016 for Community Leader, the "Extraordinary Woman's Award". She has actively participated as a volunteer in many community organizations because public service and community involvement are major aspects of her life. She has served as a volunteer with organizations such as The Latino Political Action Committee, The Latino Civic Fund, leader in married couple ministry at Praise Tabernacle Church and as an active board member of CODAC Behavioral Healthcare.

Maria Rivera

Public Relations
LLI 2014

Maria Rivera was born in Puerto Rico and became the first Puerto Rican to hold a seat in the City of Central Falls Council as Councilwoman-at-large. Mrs. Rivera is currently pursuing her education at Roger Williams university, majoring in Public Administration and works for the State of Rhode Island's Department of Human Services as a senior eligibility technician. She is an alumni of the Rhode Island Latino Leadership Institute, previously a member of the Rhode Island Latino Civic Fund and the RI Political Action Committee and the Democratic committee in Central falls. She is also a member of the Puerto Rican Professionals Association of Rhode Island. She is the mother of 2 teenagers who have motivated her to continue engaging in the professional and community projects of value.

Sylvia Bernal

RIPLA
Treasurer

Born and raised in Chiclayo, Peru, Sylvia came to the US in 1991, she holds several professional certifications as an Administrative Assistant, Marketing, Real Estate Investor and Long Term Care Specialist. She attended the Community College of RI for the Business Administration Program and is currently pursuing a Bachelors in Arts for the Organizational Leadership and Change Program at College Unbound.

A former entrepreneur, Sylvia founded Nice & Neat Cleaning Services Inc. and Sylber Properties and currently works for United Way RI as a Medicare-Medicaid Eligible Counselor. She is the Treasurer of RIPLA and has been very active in the community serving in the executive board of RILPAC, The Rhode Island Latino Civic Fund, Gateway Health Care Realty Board, Centro Cultural Andino, Peruvian Soul, Brotherhood of the Lord of Miracles among others.

Appendix

The 20th Century's Longest Revolution Still Has Work to Do

Women now matter and society has been transformed; the next generation must assume the mantle.

By RUTH ROSEN
Friday, December 31, 1999

American women entered the 20th century without the right to vote and ended it with the right "to have it all" as long as they "do it all." Progress? It depends on whom you ask. In many ways, the women's movement has been the longest revolution of the century.

Bursts of artillery fire, mass strikes, massacred protesters and bomb explosions are our usual images of revolution. Yet some revolutions are harder to recognize: No cataclysms mark their beginnings or ends, no casualties are left lying in pools of blood. Though people may suffer greatly, their pain is hidden. Such was the case with the modern women's movement. Activists didn't hurl tear gas canisters at the police or burn down buildings, overthrow the government or achieve economic dominance. They did, however, subvert authority and transform society in dramatic and irrevocable ways.

Consider the last half of the 20th century. Before the 1950s, the president of Harvard University saw no reason to increase the number of female undergraduates because the university's mission was to "train leaders." Newspaper ads separated jobs by sex. Bars often refused to serve women. Banks routinely denied women credit or loans. Some states even excluded women from jury duty. No women ran big corporations or universities, worked as firefighters, sat on the Supreme Court, climbed telephone poles or owned construction companies. All hurricanes bore female names, thanks to the widely held view that women brought chaos.

As late as 1970, Dr. Edgar Berman, a widely known physician, proclaimed on television that women were too tortured by hormonal disturbances to assume the presidency of the nation. Few people knew more than a handful of women professors, doctors or lawyers. If a woman wanted an abortion, legal nowhere in the United States, she risked her life searching among quacks in back alleys for a competent and compassionate doctor. The public believed that rape victims probably had "asked for it," and most women felt too ashamed to report it. No language existed to make sense of marital rape, date rape, domestic violence or sexual harassment. Just two words summed up the hidden injuries women suffered in silence: "That's life."

American women's participation in both the labor force and the sexual revolution had dramatically altered their lives. Yet it took the modern women's movement to address the many ways women felt exploited, to lend legitimacy to their growing sense of injustice.

Many men and women did not see change coming. In 1967, internationally renowned sociologist David Riesman, then a professor at Harvard, uttered what has to be one of the most hilarious predictions in recent history. Writing in Time magazine in 1967, he declared that "if anything remains more or less unchanged, it will be the role of women." Poor timing. That was the year the modern women's movement began spreading across the country. As women activists learned to see the world through their own eyes, the feminist movement fragmented, and new populations of women--trade unionists, the old, the young, racial and ethnic minorities, some of whom had initially spurned feminism--began to assert different priorities. Many different feminisms began permeating American society. A backlash was inevitable, though few anticipated its religious and political ferocity.

However, by the end of the 20th century, feminist ideas had burrowed too deeply into our culture for resistance or politics to root them out. The backlash, in short, reflected a society deeply divided and disturbed by rapid changes in men's and women's lives.

Yet at the height of this national debate, more American women, not fewer, grasped the importance of the goals of the women's movement. In 1986, a Gallup Poll asked women: "Do you consider yourself a feminist?" Fifty-six percent of American women answered yes.

Women of all classes were becoming aware of the ways in which gender shaped their lives. Pollsters consistently found that more African American women approved of the goals of the women's movement than did white women. A 1989 poll found that 51% of all men, 64% of white women, 72% of Latino women and 85% of African American women agreed with the statement: "The United States continues to need a strong women's movement to push for changes that benefit women."

Perhaps the most important legacy was precisely that "women's issues" had entered mainstream national politics, where they had changed the terms of political debate. Everyday life had also changed in small but significant ways. Strangers addressed a woman as Ms.; schoolchildren learned about sexism before they became teenagers; language became more gender-neutral; popular culture saturated society with comedies, thrillers and mysteries that turned on changing gender roles. And two decades after the movement's first years, the number of women politicians doubled. Even more significant, millions of women had entered jobs that once had been reserved for men. Although women had not gained the power to change institutions, they had joined men in colleges and universities in

unprecedented numbers. In the 1950s, women constituted only 20% of college undergraduates, and their two most common aspirations, according to polls, were to become the wife of a prominent man and the mother of several accomplished children. By 1990, women constituted 54% of undergraduates, and they wanted to do anything and everything.

Women also had joined men in blue-collar and professional jobs in startling numbers. In 1960, 35% of women had worked outside the home; by 1990, that figure had jumped to 58%.

The cumulative impact of decades of education, debates, controversies and high-profile trials raised women's gender consciousness, which in turn eventually showed up in a long-awaited political "gender gap." In 1871, Susan B. Anthony prematurely predicted that once women got the right to vote, they would vote as a bloc. A gender gap did not appear until 1980, when more men than women voted for Ronald Reagan, whose opposition to the Equal Rights Amendment and abortion may have moved some women into the Democratic column. Eventually the gender gap would cause at least a temporary realignment of national politics. In 1996, 16% more women than men voted for Bill Clinton for president.

Some political analysts now believed that women were voting their interests as workers, family caregivers or as single or divorced mothers. Gender gap or not, the rightward tilt of American politics led to the demonization of poor women and their children. While some middle-class women captured meaningful and well-paid work, ever more women slid into poverty and homelessness, which, on balance, the women's movement did too little, too late, to change.

Each generation of women activists leaves an unfinished agenda for the next generation. First-wave suffragists fought for women's citizenship and created international organizations dedicated to universal disarmament but left many customs and beliefs unchallenged. Second-wave feminists questioned nearly everything, transformed much of American culture, expanded the idea of democracy by insisting that equality had to include the realities of its women citizens and catapulted women's issues onto a global stage. Women now mattered.

Yet these activists left much unfinished too. They were unable to change most institutions, to gain greater economic justice for poor women or even to convince society that child care is the responsibility of the whole society. American women won the right to "have it all" but only if they "did it all."

The struggle is just beginning. It is for a new generation to identify what they need in order to achieve greater equality.

As each generation shares its secrets, women learn to see the world through their own eyes and discover, much to their surprise, that their problems are not theirs alone. The poet Muriel Requester once asked: "What would happen if one woman told the truth about her life?" Her answer: "The world would split open." And so it has. A revolution is underway, and there is no end in sight.

Rhode Island Latino Civic Fund Hispanics In Philanthropy Funding

EIN: **41-2045469**　　　　　Nonprofit Tax Code Designation: **501(c)(4)**

Defined as: Civic leagues, social welfare organizations and local associations of employees, created to promote community welfare for charitable, educational or recreational purposes.

Donations to this organization are not tax deductible.

https://projects.propublica.org/nonprofits/organizations/412045469

Hispanics In Philanthropy (HIP)

http://www.hiponline.org/programs/capacity-building/funders-collaborative-for-strong-latino-communities/fc-grantees/record/001d000000HyjCHAAZ

The Rhode Island Latino Civic Fund (RILCF) was established in 2002 with the purpose of promoting the civic education, registration, and participation of Latinos in the state of Rhode Island. In addition, the organization is actively involved in educating and informing elected officials about the issues and concerns impacting the Latino community in Rhode Island.

RILCF has remained united by its shared commitment to equality and justice. The organization strives to create a community where every Rhode Islanders has access to quality education, healthcare, housing, and livable wage jobs that support them and their respective families achieve their full potential. Furthermore, RILCF aims to accomplish its goals and overarching purpose by doing the following:

4. Promoting the participation of the Latino community in the civic life and democratic processes of Rhode Island through activities, such as those that increase voter education, voter registration and voter anticipation.

5. Raising awareness in the Latino community regarding public policy issues benefiting Latinos and other individuals from urban communities as well as those that could adversely impact the Latino community.

6. Ensuring that elected officials, political leaders and candidates have a broad understanding of the concerns and priorities among Rhode Island Latinos.

Grants Awarded

http://www.hiponline.org/grantees/grants-awarded?AccountId=001d000000HyjCH

Recipient: **Rhode Island Latino Civic Fund**
Program: **MA-RI Funders' Collaborative**
Amount: **$21,600**
Grant Start Date: **August 15, 2006**
Grant End Date: **August 14, 2007**

Recipient:	Rhode Island Latino Civic Fund
Program:	MA-RI Funders' Collaborative
Round:	Round 3 - Massachusetts/Rhode Island FC
Amount:	$21,600

Start Date: August 15, 2006

End Date: August 14, 2007

Grant Goals:

To build the organization's communications and outreach capacities by purchasing interpreting equipment to increase participation of the monolingual Latino population that has not been involved with civic issues and by hiring one or more consultants to develop a communications and marketing plan.

Recipient: **Rhode Island Latino Civic Fund**
Program: **MA-RI Funders' Collaborative**
Amount: **$23,870**
Grant Start Date: **November 15, 2007**
Grant End Date: **November 15, 2008**

Recipient: Rhode Island Latino Civic Fund

Program: MA-RI Funders' Collaborative

Round: Round 4 - Massachusetts/Rhode Island FC

Amount: $23,870

Start Date: November 15, 2007

End Date: November 15, 2008

Grant Goals:

To build the organization's planning capacity by hiring a consultant to facilitate a strategic planning process culminating in the creation of a strategic plan for the organization.

Recipient: **Rhode Island Latino Civic Fund**
Program: **MA-RI Funders' Collaborative**
Amount: **$100,000**
Grant Start Date: **August 15, 2009**
Grant End Date: **August 14, 2011**
More Grant Details

Recipient: Rhode Island Latino Civic Fund

Program: MA-RI Funders' Collaborative

Round: Round 4 - Massachusetts/Rhode Island FC

Amount: $100,000

Start Date: August 15, 2009

End Date: August 14, 2011

Grant Goals:

To build programmatic, organizational, leadership, public relations and fundraising capacities by funding activities to do the following:

1. obtain professionally produced course materials, including workbooks, slides, presentations and brochures, resulting in increased efficiency in volunteer time and the improvement of programs and services to the Latino community;

2. hire a part-time executive director to collaborate with the board in development and training to implement a strategic plan, improve internal business practices, obtain 501(c)(3) status, and develop strategic partnerships with organizations of similar purpose on the local, state and nation level, resulting in an improvement in organizational effectiveness, internal and external collaboration, and sustainability; and

3. hire a consultant to assist the board and executive director in the creation and implementation of public relations and fundraising strategies, and the enhancement of the website, resulting in increased visibility in and communication with the community and an increase in the quantity and diversification of funding sources.

Rhode Island Latino Civic Fund Bylaws

Article I   Name and Purpose

Section 1.   The name of this organization is the Rhode Island Latino Civic Fund.

Section 2.   The Rhode Island Latino Civic Fund is organized and shall be operated for the purposes of promoting civic values and social welfare within the meaning of Section 501(c)4 of the Internal Revenue Code of 1986, as amended.

Section 3.   The Rhode Island Latino Civic Fund is a nonpartisan, nonprofit organization formed to advance the following goals:

A.   To promote the participation of the Latino community in the civic life and democratic processes of Rhode Island through activities such as those that increase voter education, voter registration and voter participation.

B.   To raise awareness in the Latino community regarding public policy issues benefiting Latinos and other individuals from urban communities as well as those that could adversely impact the Latino community.

C.   To insure that elected officials, political leaders and candidates have a broad understanding of the concerns and priorities among Rhode Island Latinos.

Article II   Membership

Section 1.   Members

A.   Membership shall be open to Latinos and other persons who are at least eighteen (18) years of age and comply with the financial obligations set by the Board of Directors.

Section 2.   Types of Members:

A.   *Active*: Members who comply with the financial obligations set by the Board and regularly attend meetings.

   1. A member may lose his/her active standing if he/she has not met his/her obligation towards the Rhode Island Latino Civic Fund and/or has missed more than three (3) consecutive monthly membership meetings. After three (3) consecutive absences, the general membership will decide whether to change the Active Member's standing to Associate Member. Changes in standing will be decided by a majority vote at a regularly scheduled meeting.

B.   *Associate:* Members who comply with the financial obligations set by the Board but do not wish to regularly attend meetings. Associate Members shall be entitled to receive regular correspondence and information on the Rhode Island Latino Civic Fund's activities and programs.

   1. Associate Members may become Active Members by attending three regular monthly meetings in a row and soliciting for Active Membership at the third meeting attended.

Section 3.   Voting Rights

   A.   Only Active Members in good standing shall have the following rights:

1.   Full voting rights at all membership meetings after being in good standing for three months.

2. The right to determine and formulate all Rhode Island Latino Civic Fund fundamental policies.

3. The right to vote on any matter brought before the organization by the Board of Directors.

Section 3. Financial Obligations

A. Members shall pay an annual fee in the manner specified by the Board of Directors.

B. Annual Fees will be valid from January to December of each calendar year.

C. These fees may be changed by the Board of Directors as required, with approval of the membership.

Article III **Directors**

Section 1. Number, Election and Term of Office

The Board of Directors shall consist of no less than three (3) members elected by those members of the Rhode Island Latino Civic Fund with voting rights in the manner described in Article II, Section 3. The following officers shall be members of the Board of Directors and will constitute the Executive Board of Directors:

1. President
2. Executive Vice President
3. Vice President
4. Secretary
5. Assistant Secretary
6. Treasurer
7. Assistant Treasurer

Said officers and other elected Directors will hold office for a two (2) year term of office, elected by a majority vote of the Active Members present and voting at a duly constituted meeting called for that purpose. Thereafter, elections shall take place during the last week of November in odd years. Directors will continue to serve until their successors are elected, though this time may not exceed 60 days past the expiration date of their term of office.

Section 2. Election Procedures and Restrictions

A. The Chairperson of the Elections Committee shall be appointed by the President of the Board of Directors.

B. The Elections Committee shall be comprised of Active Members who are nominated and approved at a regular monthly meeting. Election Committee members are ineligible for nomination to officer positions.

C. Election Procedures shall be developed two (2) months prior to the November meeting by the Elections Committee. These procedures shall be reviewed and approved by a majority of the Active Members and the meeting one (1) month prior to the November elections meeting.

D. Six months of Active Membership will be required to qualify for nomination as an officer.

E. Candidates interested in being considered to positions on the Board of Directors will express their interest directly to the Elections Committee by letter or email. However, only the Elections Committee shall have the power to nominate candidates to fill expiring terms on the Board of Directors.

F. If the Election Committee is unable to garner nominations for any of the officer positions, it shall be the responsibility of the incoming President to appoint an Active Member to said vacant position. If the President is unable to fill the vacancy with an Active Member, he/she may appoint an Associate Member. Presidential appointments to vacant positions shall be subject to approval by a majority of the members at a duly constituted regular membership meeting.

G. Only Active Members in good standing at the time of the election, shall have the right to vote at said election. The Secretary of the Board will provide and certify the list of Active Members prior to votes being cast.

H.   Mid-term vacancies in the Board of Directors are to be filled by the President with approval of the membership at the next regular membership meeting. The President shall first seek to fill the vacancy with an Active Member in good standing. If said vacancy cannot be filled by an Active Member, the President may seek appointment of an Associate Member willing to become Active. Those elected in mid-term due to a vacancy shall do so until the end of said term as determined by the last General Election.

I.   Those holding the offices of President and Executive Vice President can do so for a maximum of two (2) consecutive terms.

Section 3.   Removal of Directors/Members

A.   A director or member may be removed at any time by an affirmative vote of two thirds (2/3) of the Directors then in office and voting, at a meeting properly called for that purpose.

Section 4.   Powers and Authority of Board of Directors

The Directors so designated shall constitute the Board of Directors of Rhode Island Latino Civic Fund to act in the manner and with the powers provided in these Bylaws and to further the goals as stated in our Articles of Incorporation, as amended from time to time. No Director shall represent or act on behalf of the Board of Directors without the explicit authority of the Board of Directors. Said authority to represent the Board of Directors shall be granted only after approval by a vote of the majority of the Board of Directors.

Section 5.   Vacancies

Vacant seats on the Board of Directors shall be filled for the unexpired portion of the term by a candidate selected by the President and approved by a majority vote of the Board of Directors.

Article IV   Duties of Officers

Section 1.   President

A.   The President presides at all meetings of the Rhode Island Latino Civic Fund and is an ex officio member of all committees set forth in these Bylaws.

B.   The President has the direct responsibility for implementing all policies established by Rhode Island Latino Civic Fund.

C.   The President appoints chairpersons for all committees set forth in these Bylaws and fills vacancies on all these committees with the approval of a majority of the Directors. He/she casts all tie breaking votes.

D.   The President may act as an official representative of the Rhode Island Latino Civic Fund in other political and nonpolitical organizations and performs those duties as authorized by the Board of Directors.

E.   The President is responsible for keeping in contact with the political community in the State of Rhode Island.

F.   When required, the President signs all checks along with the Treasurer, or Executive Vice President.

Section 2.   Executive Vice President

A.   The Executive Vice President assists the President in the performance of the latter's duties and assumes the full responsibilities of said office in his/her absence.

B.   The Executive Vice President assumes such additional duties as may be assigned by the President.

Section 3. Vice President

A. The Vice President assists the Executive Vice President in the performance of the latter's duties.

B. The Vice President assumes such additional duties as may be assigned by the President.

Section 4. Secretary

A. The Secretary shall record and report the minutes of all membership and Board of Director's meetings. He/she shall be responsible for the distribution of the minutes to the membership or Directors, as the case may be, at least five (5) working days prior to any meeting. He/she shall be responsible for maintaining an accurate record of all meetings.

B. The Secretary is responsible for notifying the membership and the Directors of future meetings in the manner provided in these Bylaws.

C. The Secretary is responsible for keeping attendance at all meetings, and his/her records shall be the official record of attendance. He/she shall perform other duties as assigned by the President.

Section 4. Assistant Secretary

A. The Assistant Secretary shall keep records of all of the Rhode Island Latino Civic Fund's correspondence as deemed necessary and shall be responsible for maintaining the historical archives of the organization, including press clippings, press releases, Rhode Island Latino Civic Fund columns and other ephemera produced by the organization.

B. The Assistant Secretary assists the Secretary in the performance of the latter's duties and assumes the full responsibilities of the Secretary in his/her absence. He/she shall perform other duties as assigned by the Secretary or President.

Section 5. Treasurer

A. The Treasurer receives and collects funds in accordance with the Rhode Island and United States laws and regulations. He/she shall prepare and submit any reports required by law, including annual reports to the Internal Revenue Service.

B. The Treasurer will deposit all funds in an appropriate account and pay all bills duly approved by the Board of Directors.

C. Bills due or reimbursements for duly authorized expenses by members in the amount of less than $100.00 will be paid by the Treasurer or, if so designated, the Assistant Treasurer. Bills due or reimbursements for duly authorized expenses by members in an amount greater than $100.00 shall be paid by the Treasurer or, if so designated, by the Assistant Treasurer after approval by the Executive Board of Directors.

D. The Treasurer shall present financial reports at regular membership meetings and keep accurate records of all monies received and paid out supported with appropriate documentation.

E. The Treasurer shall be the Chairperson of any committee formed by the Board of Directors for budget preparation.

Section 6. Assistant Treasurer

The Assistant Treasurer assists the Treasurer in the performance of the latter's duties and assumes the full responsibilities of the Treasurer in his/her absence. He she shall perform other duties as assigned by the Treasurer or President.

Article V   Rhode Island Latino Civic Fund Meetings

Section 1. Annual Meeting

An annual meeting of the Rhode Island Latino Civic Fund shall be held for the purpose of, the election of the Board of Directors when applicable, amending the Bylaws and the Articles of Incorporation or to transact any other business that may properly come before the meeting. Said meeting shall be held during the last week in November.

Section 2.   Regular Meetings

A.   Regular meetings of the Rhode Island Latino Civic Fund shall be held at least once every other month at such time and place as specified by the Board of Directors.

B.   Meetings of the Board of Directors shall be held at least once a month at a time and placed specified by the Board.

C.   Notice of all regular meetings shall be provided at the beginning of each calendar year. Any changes to the regular meeting calendar shall require five (5) days written notice to the membership.

Section 3.   Membership Strategic Planning Retreat

The Board of Directors shall prepare an annual membership Strategic Planning Retreat every June.

Section 3.   Special Meetings

A.   Special meetings may be called by the President and shall be called by the President upon written request of any two (2) Directors. If the President does not call the Special Meeting within five (5) workings days after receipt of said written request, the meeting may be called by the Directors making said request.

B.   At least five (5) working days of oral or written notice of each Special Meeting stating the time and place of the meeting shall be given each Director or member, as the case may be.

C.   No notice of a meeting need be given to a Director or member who attended said meeting in person without protesting prior to or at the commencement of said meeting, or who waives such notice in writing. Said waiver must be filed with the Secretary of the Rhode Island Latino Civic Fund either before or after the meeting.

Section 4.   Conduct of Meetings

A.   All meetings shall be conducted in accordance with *Robert's Rules of Order, Revised*.

Article VI   Quorum and Voting Requirements

Section 1.   Quorum for transaction of business

A majority (51%) of the Active Members shall constitute a quorum for the transaction of business at meeting.

Section 2.   Quorum for approval of actions
The affirmative vote of a majority of Active Members present at the meeting at which a quorum is present shall be required for action by the Rhode Island Latino Civic Fund or the Board of Directors on any matter.

Article VII   Committees

Section 1.   Standing Committees
The Rhode Island Latino Civic Fund may have the following standing committees:

- Outreach – responsible for voter education, registration and participation
- Development – responsible for fundraising activities
- Elections – created on Election years in accordance with Article III, Section 2.

Section 2.   Other Committees
A.   The Board of Directors by majority vote may designate other committees as it may deem appropriate.

B.   All committees shall be required to present reports to the membership as requested by the President or a majority of the directors.

The standing committees and other committees designated by the Board of Directors may have and exercise only such authority as is expressly provided by resolution from the Board of Directors creating such committees. Each committee shall serve at the pleasure of the Board of Directors and must keep minutes of its meetings.

Article VIII Amendments

Section 1. By-Laws

A. Amendments to the By-Laws must be presented to the membership for consideration in writing during the week prior to the meeting at which the amendment will be considered.

B. By-Laws can be amended only by a two-thirds (2/3) vote of those Active Members in good standing present and voting at a properly called regular meeting.

C. If any provision of these By-Laws is found to be inconsistent with any provision of the Articles of Incorporation, as it presently exists, or as from time to time amended, the former shall constitute the controlling authority.

Article IX Distribution of Assets

Section 1. No part of the income or assets of the Rhode Island Latino Civic Fund shall be distributed to a Director or member.

Section 2. Upon dissolution of the Rhode Island Latino Civic Fund, the assets remaining after payment of all liabilities shall be distributed to the Rhode Island Foundation to promote activities that fulfill the original goals of the Rhode Island Latino Civic Fund.

Article X Seal

The Seal of the Rhode Island Latino Civic Fund shall be a circular seal, with the name of the Organization and words "Seal" and "Rhode Island" set forth therein. The Secretary shall have custody of the seal.

Certified as the amended By-Laws of the Rhode Island Latino Civic Fund adopted at a meeting of the Organization on the **16th day of July, 2002**.

_____
Secretary
501 (c4)

https://www.irs.gov/pub/irs-tege/eotopicl03.pdf

I To be tax-exempt as a social welfare organization described in Internal Revenue Code (IRC) section 501(c)(4), an organization must not be organized for profit and must be operated exclusively to promote social welfare. The earnings of a section 501(c)(4) organization may not inure to the benefit of any private shareholder or individual. If the organization engages in an excess benefit transaction with a person having substantial influence over the organization, an excise tax may be imposed on the person and any managers agreeing to the transaction. See Introduction to IRC 4958 for more information about this excise tax. For a more detailed discussion of the exemption requirements for section 501(c)(4) organizations, see IRC 501(c)(4) Organizations. For more information about applying for exemption, see Application for Recognition of Exemption.

To be operated exclusively to promote social welfare, an organization must operate primarily to further the common good and general welfare of the people of the community (such as by bringing about civic betterment and social improvements). For example, an organization that restricts the use of its facilities to employees of selected corporations and their guests is primarily benefiting a private group rather than the community and, therefore, does not qualify as a section 501(c)(4) organization. Similarly, an organization formed to represent member-tenants of an apartment complex does not qualify, because its activities benefit the member-tenants and not all tenants in the community, while an organization formed to promote the legal rights of all tenants in a particular community may qualify under section 501(c)(4) as a social welfare organization. An organization is not operated primarily for the promotion of social welfare if its primary activity is operating a social club for the benefit, pleasure or recreation of its members, or is carrying on a business with the general public in a manner similar to organizations operated for profit link].

Seeking legislation germane to the organization's programs is a permissible means of attaining social welfare purposes. Thus, a section 501(c)(4) social welfare organization may further its exempt purposes through lobbying as its primary activity without jeopardizing its exempt status. An organization that has lost its section 501(c)(3) status due to substantial attempts to influence legislation may not thereafter qualify as a section 501(c)(4) organization. In addition, a section 501(c)(4) organization that engages in lobbying may be required to either provide notice to its members regarding the percentage of dues paid that are applicable to lobbying activities or pay a proxy tax. For more information, see Lobbying Issues .

The promotion of social welfare does not include direct or indirect participation or intervention in political campaigns on behalf of or in opposition to any candidate for public office. However, a section 501(c)(4) social welfare organization may engage in some political activities, so long as that is not its primary activity. However, any expenditure it makes for political activities may be subject to tax under section 527(f). For further information regarding political and lobbying activities of section 501(c) organizations, see Election Year Issues, Political Campaign and Lobbying Activities of IRC 501(c)(4), (c)(5), and (c)(6) Organizations, and Revenue Ruling 2004-6.

Rhode Island Latino Civic Fund Incorporation

ID Number: 000125204

Summary for: RHODE ISLAND LATINO CIVIC FUND

The exact name of the Domestic Non-Profit Corporation: RHODE ISLAND LATINO CIVIC FUND

Entity type: Domestic Nonprofit Corporation

Identification Number: 000125204

Date of Incorporation in Rhode Island: 06-11-2002

Latina Politics, Latino Politics: Gender, Culture, and Political Participation in Boston

Purpose: To Promote The Participation Of The Latino Community In The Civic Life And Democratic Processes Of Rhode Island Title: 7-6

Rhode Island Department of State
Nellie M. Gorbea
Secretary of State

HOME | BUSINESS PORTAL | ELECTIONS | CIVICS AND EDUCATION

Entity Summary

ID Number: 000125204

[Request certificate] [New search]

Summary for: RHODE ISLAND LATINO CIVIC FUND

The exact name of the Domestic Non-Profit Corporation:	RHODE ISLAND LATINO CIVIC FUND
Entity type:	Domestic Non-Profit Corporation
Identification Number:	000125204
Date of Incorporation in Rhode Island: 06-11-2002	**Effective Date:** 06-11-2002

The location of the Principal Office:

Address: 127 DORRANCE STREET, 4TH FLOOR
City or Town, State, Zip, Country: PROVIDENCE, RI 02903 USA

Agent Resigned: N   Address Maintained: Y

The name and address of the Registered Agent:

Name: JOSEPH MOLINA FLYNN
Address: 127 DORRANCE STREET, 4TH FLOOR
City or Town, State, Zip, Country: PROVIDENCE, RI 02903 USA

The Officers and Directors of the Corporation:

Title	Individual Name	Address
PRESIDENT	JOSEPH MOLINA FLYNN	127 DORRANCE STREET, 4TH FLOOR PROVIDENCE, RI 02903 USA
TREASURER	WESLEY RODAS	136 CHANDLER AVENUE PAWTUCKET, RI 02860 USA
SECRETARY	PATRICIA SOCARRAS	144 PARKVIEW DR APT 35 PAWTUCKET, RI 02861 USA
VICE PRESIDENT	MARCELA BETANCUR	28 MAY STREET NORTH PROVIDENCE, RI 02904 USA
DIRECTOR	DIANA PERDOMO	1565 MAIN ROAD TIVERTON, RI 02878 USA
DIRECTOR	LUANNE SANTELISES	222 RESERVOIR AVE PROVIDENCE, RI 02907 USA

Purpose:

TO PROMOTE THE PARTICIPATION OF THE LATINO COMMUNITY IN THE CIVIC LIFE AND DEMOCRATIC PROCESSES OF RHODE ISLAND
TITLE: 7-6

North American Industry Classification System Code(NAICS):

813990 Other Similar Organizations (except Business, Professional, Labor, and Political Organizations)

View filings for this business entity:

ALL FILINGS

Click here to access 2006 and 2007 annual reports filed prior to July 25, 2007. The corporate ID is required.

[View filings]

[New search]

Filing Fee: $35.00

ID Number: 1252

STATE OF RHODE ISLAND AND PROVIDENCE PLANTATIONS
Office of the Secretary of State
Corporations Division
100 North Main Street
Providence, Rhode Island 02903-1335

NON-PROFIT CORPORATION

ARTICLES OF INCORPORATION
(To Be Filed In Duplicate Original)

The undersigned, acting as incorporator(s) of a corporation under Chapter 7-6 of the General Laws, 1956, as amen adopt(s) the following Articles of Incorporation for such corporation:

1. The name of the corporation is   Rhode Island Latino Civic Fund

2. The period of its duration is (if perpetual, so state)   Perpetual

3. The specific purpose or purposes for which the corporation is organized are:

   To promote the participation of the Latino community in the civic life and democratic processes of Rhode Island through activities such as those that increase voter education, voter registration and voter participation.

   To raise awareness in the Latino community regarding public policy issues benefiting Latinos and other individuals from communities as well as those that could adversely impact the Latino community.

   To insure that elected and appointed officials, political leaders and candidates for public office have a broad understanding of the concerns and priorities amonth RI Latinos.

4. Provisions, if any, not inconsistent with the law, which the incorporators elect to set forth in these article incorporation for the regulation of the internal affairs of the corporation are:

   See Attachment 1.

Form No. 200
Revised: 01/99

FILED
JUN 1 1 2002
By AHF
284931

5. The address of the initial registered office of the corporation is **400 Moosehorn Road**
(Street Address, *not* P.O. Box)

East Greenwich, RI **02818**, and the name of its initial registered agent at su(
(City/Town)   (Zip Code)

address is **Nellie M. Gorbea**
(Name of Agent)

6. The number of directors constituting the initial Board of Directors of the Corporation is **Seven (7)**
(not less than three directors)

and the names and addresses of the persons who are to serve as the initial directors are:

Name	Address
Nellie M. Gorbea, President	400 Moosehorn Road East Greenwich, RI 02818-1114
Melba Depena, Executive Vice Presid	9 Eighth Street Providence, RI 02906
Tony Affigne, Vice President	7 Nicholas Brown Yard Providence, RI 02904
Sylvia M. Bernal, Treasurer	30 Vernon Street Providence, RI 02903
Domingo Morel, Assistant Treasurer	79 Ivan Street, Apt. 27 North Providence, RI 02904
Ana-Cecilia Rosado, Secretary	546 Angell Street Appt. B2, Providence RI 02906

Claudia K. Cardona, Assistant Sec. 97 Robin Hollow Rd. West Greenwich, RI 02

7. The name and address of each incorporator is:

Name	Address
Michael Aaronson	1604 Broad Street Cranston, RI 02905

8. Date when corporate existence is to begin **Upon the filing of these papers.**
(not prior to, nor more than 30 days after, the filing of these Articles of Incorporatic

Under penalty of perjury, I/we declare and affirm that I/we have examined these Articles of Incorporation, including an accompanying attachments, and that all statements containe herein are true and correct.

Date: 6-10-02

Signature of each Incorporator

Attachment 1

RHODE ISLAND LATINO CIVIC FUND

ARTICLES OF INCORPORATION
ARTICLE FOURTH

Said corporation is organized exclusively for educational and civic purposes, as specified in Section 501 (c) (4) of the Internal Revenue Code of 1986.

No part of the net earnings of the corporation shall inure to the benefit of, or be distributed to, its members, trustees, or other private persons, except that the corporation shall be authorized and empowered to pay reasonable compensation for services rendered and to make payments and distributions in furtherance of the purposes set forth in Article third hereof.

Upon the dissolution of the corporation, the officers shall, after paying or making provisions for the payment of all of the liabilities of the corporation, dispose of all assets of the corporation exclusively for the purposes of the corporation in such manner, or to such organization or organizations established and operated exclusively for charitable or educational purposes as shall at the time qualify as an exempt organization or organizations under section 501 (c) (3) of the Internal Revenue Code of 1986 (or the corresponding provision of any United States Revenue Law), as the officers shall determine. Any such assets not so disposed of shall be disposed of by the Superior Court of the county in which the principal office of the corporation is then located, exclusively for such purposes.

Filing Fee: $10.00

ID Number: 125204

STATE OF RHODE ISLAND AND PROVIDENCE PLANTATIONS
Office of the Secretary of State
Corporations Division
100 North Main Street
Providence, Rhode Island 02903-1335

NON-PROFIT CORPORATION

**STATEMENT OF CHANGE OF REGISTERED AGENT
BY THE CORPORATION**

Pursuant to the provisions of Sections 7-6-13 or 7-6-78 of the General Laws, 1956, as amended, the undersigned corporation submits the following statement for the purpose of changing its registered agent and its registered office in the state of Rhode Island:

1. The name of the corporation is **RHODE ISLAND LATINO CIVIC FUND**

2. The address of the registered office as PRESENTLY shown in the corporate records on file with the Rhode Island Secretary of State is: **400 HOOSEHORN RD. RI 02818 East Greenwich**

3. The address of the NEW registered office is: **61 TAPPAN ST PROVIDENCE RI 02908**

4. The name of the registered agent as PRESENTLY shown in the corporate records on file with the Rhode Island Secretary of State is: **NELLIE GORBEA**

5. The name of the NEW registered agent is **TOMAS AVILA**

6. The address of the corporation's registered office and the address of the office of its registered agent, as changed, will be identical.

7. The change was authorized by resolution duly adopted by its board of directors.

Date: **8/3/04**

Under penalty of perjury, I declare that the information contained herein is true and correct.

RI Latino Civic Fund
Print Corporate Name

By _____
Its President ☑ or Its Vice President ☐

FILED
AUG 16 2004
By _____

Form No. 641
Revised 06/01

STATE OF RHODE ISLAND AND PROVIDENCE PLANTATIONS
Office of the Secretary of State

Matthew A. Brown, *Secretary of State*
Corporations Division
148 W. River Street
Providence, RI 02904-2615
401-222-3040

NON-PROFIT CORPORATION ANNUAL REPORT FOR THE YEAR 2005

Filing Period: June 1 - June 30 • Filing Fee: $20.00
* In accordance with R.I.G.L. 7-6-91, each corporation failing or refusing to file its annual report within the time prescribed by law (R.I.G.L. 7-6-91) is subject to a penalty fee of $25.00.

1. Corporate ID No: **125204**
2. Name of Corporation: **RHODE ISLAND LATINO CIVIC FUND**
3. State of Incorporation: **RHODE ISLAND**
4. Corporate address in Rhode Island - Street Address: **P.O. BOX 023023**, City: **PROVIDENCE**, Zip: **02903**
5. Foreign corporation: (enter principal office address)

6. Brief Description of the character of the affairs which are actually conducted by the Rhode Island corporation: **TO PROMOTE THE PARTICIPATION OF THE LATINO COMMUNITY IN THE CIVIC LIFE AND DEMOCRATIC PROCESSES OF RHODE ISLAND**

7. NAMES AND ADDRESSES OF THE OFFICERS: ("X" BOX FOR ATTACHMENT) ☐ FILL IN SPACES BEFORE USING ATTACHMENTS

President Name: **DOMINGO MOREL**	Vice President Name: **SABINA MATOS**
Street Address: **104 CANTON ST**	Street Address: **55 FLORENCE ST**
City: **PROVIDENCE** State: **RI** Zip: **02908**	City: **PROVIDENCE** State: **RI** Zip: **02909**
Secretary Name: **LAHNIS VARGAS**	Treasurer Name: **SYLVIA M. BERNAL**
Street Address: **37 CATO ST**	Street Address: **26 VERNON ST**
City: **PAWTUCKET** State: **RI** Zip: **02860**	City: **PROVIDENCE** State: **RI** Zip: **02903**

8. NAMES AND ADDRESSES OF THE DIRECTORS: ("X" BOX FOR ATTACHMENT) ☐ FILL IN SPACES BEFORE USING ATTACHMENTS
THE NUMBER OF DIRECTORS OF A DOMESTIC (RHODE ISLAND) CORPORATION **SHALL NOT BE LESS THAN THREE** (3). R.I.G.L. 7-6-23

Director Name: **NICK FIGUEROA**	Director Name: **CHRISTIAN VARGAS**
Street Address: **16 DURHAM**	Street Address: **37 CATO ST**
City: **PROVIDENCE** State: **RI** Zip: **02908**	City: **PAWTUCKET** State: **RI** Zip: **02860**
Director Name: **ANA C. ROSADO**	Director Name: **JUAN PICHARDO**
Street Address: **546 ANGEL ST APT B-2**	Street Address: **229 ATLANTIC ST**
City: **PROVIDENCE** State: **RI** Zip: **02906**	City: **PROVIDENCE** State: **RI** Zip: **02907**

9. REGISTERED AGENT IN RHODE ISLAND - DO NOT ALTER - Changes require filing of Form 641 - R.I.G.L. 7-6-13 / 7-6-78

Agent Name:
Address:

This report must be signed by either the President, Vice President, Secretary, Assistant Secretary, Treasurer, Receiver or Trustee

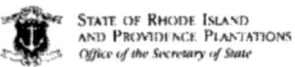

FILED
File Date: **MAY 24 2006**
Claim No:
By: **11025**
FOR SECRETARY OF STATE USE ONLY

Under penalty of perjury, I declare and affirm that I have examined this report, including any accompanying schedules and statements, and that all statements contained herein are true and correct.

Signature of Officer: *Sylvia Bernal* Date: **4/27/06**
Print or Type Name of Officer: **SYLVIA M. BERNAL**
Title of Officer: **TREASURER**

Form 631 Rev. 12/05

STATE OF RHODE ISLAND AND PROVIDENCE PLANTATIONS
Office of the Secretary of State
Matthew A. Brown, Secretary of State

Corporations Division
100 North Main Street
Providence, RI 02903-1335
401.222.3040

NON-PROFIT CORPORATION ANNUAL REPORT FOR THE YEAR 2004

Filing Period: June 1 - June 30 • Filing Fee: $20.00
(FORM MUST BE TYPED OR PRINTED IN BLACK)

1. Corporate ID No: **125204**
2. Name of Corporation: **Rhode Island Latino Civic Fund**
3. State of Incorporation: **RHODE ISLAND**
4. Corporate address in Rhode Island - Street Address: ~~P.O. BOX 23028~~ **61 Tappan Street** City: **PROVIDENCE** Zip: **02908**
5. Foreign corporations: Enter principal office address.

6. Brief Description of the character of the affairs which are actually conducted in Rhode Island:
   TO PROMOTE THE PARTICIPATION OF THE LATINO COMMUNITY IN THE CIVIC LIFE AND DEMOCRATIC PROCESSES OF RHODE ISLAND

7. NAMES AND ADDRESSES OF THE OFFICERS:

	President	Vice-President
Name	TOMAS AVILA	DOMINGO MOREL
Street	61 TAPPAN ST	79 IVAN ST APT. 27
City/State/Zip	PROVIDENCE RI 02908	NORTH PROV. RI 02904
	Secretary	Treasurer
Name	KATHERINE HELLWIG	SYLVIA BERNAL
Street	77 SEAMANS ST.	26 VERNON ST
City/State/Zip	PROVIDENCE RI 02908	PROVIDENCE RI 02903

8. NAMES AND ADDRESSES OF THE DIRECTORS:

Director Name	Street Address	City	State	Zip
Tony Affigne		PROVIDENCE	RI	
ALBERTO CARDONA	99 ROBIN HOLLOW DRIVE	N. GREENWICH	RI	02817
SABINA MATOS	33 FLORENCE ST.	PROVIDENCE	RI	02909
CARMEN MIRABAL	35 RAND ST	CENTRAL FALLS	RI	02863

9. REGISTERED AGENT IN RHODE ISLAND - DO NOT ALTER

Agent Name: ~~NELLIE M. CORDEA~~ **TOMAS A. AVILA**
Address: ~~400 MOOSEHORN ROAD~~ **61 TAPPAN ST.** City: **PROVIDENCE** ~~EAST GREENWICH~~ Zip: **02908** ~~02818~~

File Date: 10-25-04
Check No: 1062
By: a

Signature of Officer: [signed] 7/19/04
Print or Type Name of Officer: **SYLVIA M. BERNAL**
Title of Officer: **TREASURER**

Form 631 Rev. 04/04

STATE OF RHODE ISLAND AND PROVIDENCE PLANTATIONS
Office of the Secretary of State

Matthew A. Brown, Secretary of State
Corporations Division
100 North Main Street, Providence, RI 02903-1335
401.222.3040

NON-PROFIT CORPORATION ANNUAL REPORT FOR THE YEAR 2003
Filing Period: June 1 - June 30 • Filing Fee: $20.00
(FORM MUST BE TYPED OR PRINTED IN BLACK)

1. Corporate ID No.	2. Name of Corporation				
125204	Rhode Island Latino Civic Fund				
3. State of Incorporation	4. Corporate address in Rhode Island - Street Address			City	Zip
RHODE ISLAND	P.O. BOX 023023			PROVIDENCE	02903
5. Foreign corporation. Enter principal office address			City	State	Zip

6. Brief Description of the character of the affairs which are actually conducted in Rhode Island.
TO PROMOTE THE PARTICIPATION OF THE LATINO COMMUNITY IN THE CIVIC LIFE AND DEMOCRATIC PROCESSES OF RHODE ISLAND

7. NAMES AND ADDRESSES OF THE OFFICERS ("X" BOX FOR ATTACHMENT) ☐ FILL IN SPACES BEFORE USING ATTACHMENTS

President Name			Vice President Name		
HELBA DE PEÑA			MERCEDES BERNAL		
Street Address			Street Address		
60 CUNERFORD ST			27 CUNERFORD		
City	State	Zip	City	State	Zip
PROVIDENCE	RI	02909	PROVIDENCE	RI	02909
Secretary Name			Treasurer Name		
ANA CECILIA ROSADO			SYLVIA M. BERNAL		
Street Address			Street Address		
546 ANGELL ST			26 VERNON		
City	State	Zip	City	State	Zip
PROVIDENCE	RI	02906	PROVIDENCE	RI	02903

8. NAMES AND ADDRESSES OF THE DIRECTORS ("X" BOX FOR ATTACHMENT) ☐ FILL IN THE SPACES BEFORE USING ATTACHMENTS
THE NUMBER OF DIRECTORS OF A DOMESTIC (RHODE ISLAND) CORPORATION SHALL NOT BE LESS THAN THREE (3). R.I.G.L. 7-6-23

9. REGISTERED AGENT IN RHODE ISLAND - DO NOT ALTER - Changes require filing of Form 641 - R.I.G.L. 7-6-13 / 7-6-78

Agent Name	Address		
NELLIE M. GORBEA			
Address	City		Zip
400 MOOSEHORN ROAD	EAST GREENWICH		02818

This report must be signed in ink by either the President, Vice President, Secretary, Assistant Secretary, Treasurer, Receiver or Trustee

File Date **RECEIVED**
Check No. APR 0 2 2004
By: 110 1060
FOR SECRETARY OF STATE USE ONLY

Under penalty of perjury, I declare and affirm that I have examined this report, including any accompanying schedules and statements, and that all statements contained herein are true and correct.

Signature of Officer: [signed]   Date: 3/26/04
Print or Type Name of Officer: SYLVIA M. BERNAL
Title of Officer: TREASURER

Form 631 Rev. 6/02

Filing Fee: $10.00   ID Number: 125204

STATE OF RHODE ISLAND AND PROVIDENCE PLANTATIONS
Office of the Secretary of State
Corporations Division
148 W. River Street
Providence, Rhode Island 02904-2615

FILED
JUN 0 6 2006
By: _____

NON-PROFIT CORPORATION

STATEMENT OF CHANGE OF REGISTERED AGENT
BY THE CORPORATION

Pursuant to the provisions of Sections 7-6-13 or 7-6-78 of the General Laws, 1956, as amended, the undersigned corporation submits the following statement for the purpose of changing its registered agent and its registered office in the state of Rhode Island.

1. The name of the corporation is RHODE ISLAND LATINO CIVIC FUND

2. The address of the registered office as PRESENTLY shown in the corporate records on file with the Rhode Island Secretary of State is:
   61 TAPPAN ST. PROVIDENCE, RI 0290

3. The address of the NEW registered office is: 104 CANTON ST PROVIDANCE, RI 02903
   P.O. BOX 023028 PROVIDENCE, RI 02903

4. The name of the registered agent as PRESENTLY shown in the corporate records on file with the Rhode Island Secretary of State is:
   TOMAS AVILA

5. The name of the NEW registered agent is:
   DOMINGO MOREL

6. The address of the corporation's registered office and the address of the office of its registered agent, as changed, will be identical.

7. The change was authorized by resolution duly adopted by its board of directors.

Under penalty of perjury, I declare that the information contained herein is true and correct.

Date 04/27/06

Rhode Island Latino Civic Fund · Domingo Morel
Print Corporate Name

By _____
Its President [✓] or Its Vice President [ ]

Form No. 641
Revised 12/05

State of Rhode Island and Providence Plantations
Office of the Secretary of State

Fee: $20.00

Corporations Division
148 W. River Street
Providence, Rhode Island 02904-2615
Telephone: (401) 222-3040

Non-Profit Corporation
Annual Report
Filing Period: June 1 - June 30

In accordance with R.I.G.L. 7-6-94, each corporation failing or refusing to file its annual report within the time prescribed by law (R.I.G.L. 7-6-91) is subject to a penalty fee of $25.00.

ANNUAL REPORT YEAR: 2008

1. Corporate ID No. 000125204

2. Name of Corporation Rhode Island Latino Civic Fund

3. State of Incorporation

State: RI

4. Corporate Address in Rhode Island

No. and Street: PO BOX 023040
City or Town: PROVIDENCE   State: RI   Zip: 02903 Country: USA

5. Foreign Corporation. Enter Principal Office Address

No. and Street:

City or Town: State: Zip: Country:

6. Brief Description of the Character of the Affairs Which are Actually Conducted in Rhode Island

TO PROMOTE THE PARTICIPATION OF THE LATINO COMMUNITY IN THE CIVIC LIFE AND DEMOCRATIC PROCESSES OF RHODE ISLAND

7. Names and Addresses of the Officers and Directors:

THE NUMBER OF DIRECTORS OF A DOMESTIC(RHODE ISLAND)CORPORATION SHALL NOT BE LESS THAN THREE(3). R.I.G.L. 7-6-23

Title	Individual Name	Address
	First, Middle, Last, Suffix	Address, City or Town, State, Zip Code, Country
SECRETARY	ANA-CECILIA ROSADO	546 ANGELL ST. B-2 PROVIDENCE, RI 02906 USA
PRESIDENT	SABINA MATOS	35 FLORENCE STREET PROVIDENCE, RI 02909- USA
VICE PRESIDENT	DORIS DE LOS SANTOS	61 DEWEY ST. PROVIDENCE, RI 02909 USA
EXECUTIVE ASSISTANT TO THE BOARD	DORIS S BLANCHARD	18 CLIFTON RD. BRISTOL, RI 02809 USA
DIRECTOR	DR. ANTHONY AFFIGNE	61 THOMAS OLNEY COMMON PROVIDENCE, RI 02904 USA
DIRECTOR	LIZANDRA RIOJAS	P.O. BOX PROVIDENCE, RI 02903 USA
DIRECTOR	DORMINGO MOREL	290 LEGION WAY CRANSTON, RI 02910 USA
DIRECTOR	NICK FIGUEROA	16 DURHAM ST. PROVIDENCE, RI 02908 USA
DIRECTOR	VLADIMIR IBARRA	P.O. BOX 1598 PAWTUCKET, RI 02862 USA

8. REGISTERED AGENT IN RHODE ISLAND - DO NOT ALTER
Changes Require Filing of Form 641 - R.I.G.L. 7-6-13 / 7-6-78

DOMINGO MOREL 104 CANTON STREET P.O. BOX 023028 PROVIDENCE , RI 02903-

9. This report must be signed by either the President, Vice President, Secretary, Assistant Secretary, Treasurer, Receiver, or Trustee.

Signed this 30 Day of June, 2008 at 2:45:48 PM by the incorporator(s). *This electronic signature of the individual or individuals signing this instrument constitutes the affirmation or acknowledgement of the signatory, under penalties of perjury, that this instrument is that individual's act and deed or the act and deed of the corporation, and that the facts stated herein are true, as of the date of the electronic filing, in compliance with R.I. Gen. Laws § 7-1.2.*

By **SABINA MATOS**
Signature of Officer of the Corporation

X President or   __ Vice President or   __ Secretary or   __ Assistant Secretary or

__ Treasurer or   __ Receiver or   __ Trustee   (check one)

Form No. 631
Revised 09/07

RI SOS Filing Number: 200947904340 Date: 06/30/2009 10:24 PM

State of Rhode Island and Providence Plantations
Office of the Secretary of State

Fee: $20.00

Corporations Division
148 W. River Street
Providence, Rhode Island 02904-2615
Telephone: (401) 222-3040

Non-Profit Corporation
Annual Report
Filing Period: June 1 - June 30

In accordance with R.I.G.L. 7-6-94, each corporation failing or refusing to file its annual report within the time prescribed by law (R.I.G.L. 7-6-91) is subject to a penalty fee of $25.00.

ANNUAL REPORT YEAR: 2009

1. Corporate ID No. 000125204

2. Name of Corporation Rhode Island Latino Civic Fund

3. State of Incorporation

State: RI

4. Corporate Address in Rhode Island

No. and Street: PO BOX 23040
City or Town: PROVIDENCE   State: RI   Zip: 02903 Country: USA

5. Foreign Corporation. Enter Principal Office Address

No. and Street:

City or Town: State: Zip: Country:

6. Brief Description of the Character of the Affairs Which are Actually Conducted in Rhode Island

TO PROMOTE THE PARTICIPATION OF THE LATINO COMMUNITY IN THE CIVIC LIFE AND DEMOCRATIC PROCESSES OF RHODE ISLAND

7. Names and Addresses of the Officers and Directors:

All officers and directors must be listed. If officers and/or directors have been elected, the title Incorporator is no longer applicable; please delete

THE NUMBER OF DIRECTORS OF A DOMESTIC(RHODE ISLAND)CORPORATION SHALL NOT BE LESS THAN THREE(3). R.I.G.L. 7-6-23

Title	Individual Name	Address
	First, Middle, Last, Suffix	Address, City or Town, State, Zip Code, Country
PRESIDENT	DORIS M. DE LOS SANTOS	61 DEWEY STREET PROVIDENCE, RI 02909 USA
TREASURER	BELKISS LUNA-SUAZO	230 ROGER WILLIAMS AVENUE PROVIDENCE, RI 02907 USA
SECRETARY	CARMEN DIAZ-JUSINO	80 BOWLET STREET PROVIDENCE, RI 02909 USA
VICE PRESIDENT	YSA LUNA	167 ROGER WILLIAMS AVENUE PROVIDENCE, RI 02907 USA
EXECUTIVE ASSISTANT	YASMIN RINCON	104 LUBEC STREET PROVIDENCE, RI 02904 USA
DIRECTOR	SABINA MATOS	35 FLORENCE STREET PROVIDENCE, RI 02909 USA
DIRECTOR	DOMINGO MOREL	290 LEGION WAY CRANSTON, RI 02910 USA
DIRECTOR	IVETTE LUNA	27 FISK STREET PROVIDENCE, RI 02905 USA
DIRECTOR	LIZANDRA ROJAS	P.O. BOX PROVIDENCE, RI 02903 USA
DIRECTOR	OBED PAPP	88 DEXTER STREET PROVIDENCE, RI 02909 USA

8. REGISTERED AGENT IN RHODE ISLAND - DO NOT ALTER
Changes Require Filing of Form 641 - R.I.G.L. 7-6-13 / 7-6-78

DOMINGO MOREL 104 CANTON STREET P.O. BOX 023028 PROVIDENCE , RI 02903-

9. This report must be signed by either the President, Vice President, Secretary, Assistant Secretary, Treasurer, Receiver, or Trustee.

Signed this 30 Day of June, 2009 at 10:27:44 PM. *This electronic signature of the individual or individuals signing this instrument constitutes the affirmation or acknowledgement of the signatory, under penalties of perjury, that this instrument is that individual's act and deed or the act and deed of the corporation, and that the facts stated herein are true, as of the date of the electronic filing, in compliance with R.I. Gen. Laws § 7-6.*

By DORIS M. DE LOS SANTOS
Signature of Officer of the Corporation

X President or ___ Vice President or ___ Secretary or ___ Assistant Secretary or

___ Treasurer or ___ Receiver or ___ Trustee (check one)

This report cannot be accepted for filing if an officer has executed the form and he/she is not listed in Section 7.

Form No. 631
Revised 09/07

State of Rhode Island and Providence Plantations
Office of the Secretary of State

Fee: $10.00

Division Of Business Services
148 W. River Street
Providence RI 02904-2615
(401) 222-3040

Non-Profit Corporation
Articles of Amendment
(Section 7-6-40 of the General Laws of Rhode Island, 1956, as amended)

ARTICLE I

The name of the corporation is   Rhode Island Latino Civic Fund

If the entity's name is changing, state the new name: Rhode Island Latino Civic Fund

ARTICLE II

If the corporate duration is changing, so state: **X** Perpetual   ___

If the corporate purpose is changing, so state:

TO PROMOTE THE PARTICIPATION OF THE LATINO COMMUNITY IN THE CIVIC LIFE AND DEMOCRATIC PROCESSES OF RHODE ISLAND

If there is a change in the number of directors, modify this section:

The number of directors constituting the Board of Directors of the Corporation is

and the names and addresses of the persons who are to serve as the directors are:

Title	Individual Name First, Middle, Last, Suffix	Address Address, City or Town, State, Zip Code, Country
PRESIDENT	DORIS M. DE LOS SANTOS	61 DEWEY STREET PROVIDENCE, RI 02909 USA
SECRETARY	CARMEN DIAZ-JUSINO	80 BOWLET STREET PROVIDENCE, RI 02909 USA
VICE PRESIDENT	YSA LUNA	167 ROGER WILLIAMS AVENUE PROVIDENCE, RI 02907 USA
EXECUTIVE ASSISTANT	OBED PAPP	88 DEXTER STREET PROVIDENCE, RI 02909 USA
DIRECTOR	BELKISS LUNA-SUAZO	230 ROGER WILLIAMS AVE PROVIDENCE, RI 02907 USA
DIRECTOR	MICHAEL NINA	299 PROMENADE PROVIDENCE, RI 02908 USA
DIRECTOR	DOMINGO MOREL	290 LEGION WAY CRANSTON, RI 02910 USA

If there are any other provisions to be amended, so state:

ARTICLE III

The Amendment was adopted in the following manner:

(check one box only)

__X__ The amendment was adopted at a meeting of members held on 5/31/2010 , at which meeting a quorum was present, and the amendment received at least a majority of the votes which members present or represented by proxy at such meeting were entitled to cast.

___ The amendment was adopted by a consent in writing on , signed by all members entitled to vote with respect thereto.

___ The amendment was adopted at a meeting of the Board of Directors held on , and received the vote of a majority of the directors in office, there being no members entitled to vote with respect thereto.

ARTICLE IV

Date when amendment is to become effective 7/15/2010
(not prior to, nor more than 30 days after, the filing of these Articles of Amendment)

Signed this 8 Day of July, 2010 at 6:57:34 AM. *This electronic signature of the individual or individuals signing this instrument constitutes the affirmation or acknowledgement of the signatory, under penalties of perjury, that this instrument is that individual's act and deed or the act and deed of the corporation, and that the facts stated herein are true, as of the date of the electronic filing, in compliance with R.I. Gen. Laws § 7-6.*

Rhode Island Latino Civic Fund
    Corporate Name

By DORIS M. DE LOS SANTOS

   __X__ President or ___ Vice President   (check one)

AND

By CARMEN DIAZ-JUSINO

   __X__ Secretary or ___ Assistant Secretary   (check one)

Form No. 201
Revised 09/07

© 2007 - 2010 State of Rhode Island and Providence Plantations
All Rights Reserved

RI SOS   Filing Number: 201064638400   Date: 07/08/2010 6:55 AM

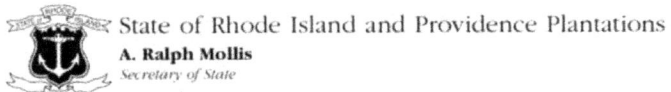 State of Rhode Island and Providence Plantations
A. Ralph Mollis
Secretary of State

STATE OF RHODE ISLAND AND PROVIDENCE PLANTATIONS

I, A. RALPH MOLLIS, Secretary of State of the State of Rhode Island and Providence Plantations, hereby certify that this document, duly executed in accordance with the provisions of Title 7 of the General Laws of Rhode Island, as amended, has been filed in this office on this day:
July 08, 2010 6:55 AM

A. Ralph Mollis

A. RALPH MOLLIS
Secretary of State

0-4401-0

RI SOS Filing Number: 201064638590 Date: 07/08/2010 7:11 AM

State of Rhode Island and Providence Plantations
Office of the Secretary of State

Fee: $10.00

Division Of Business Services
148 W. River Street
Providence RI 02904-2615
(401) 222-3040

Non-Profit Corporation
Statement of Change of Registered Agent by the Corporation
(Section 7-6-78 of the General Laws of Rhode Island, 1956, as amended)

SECTION I

The name of the corporation is Rhode Island Latino Civic Fund

SECTION II

The address of the registered office as PRESENTLY shown in the corporate records on file with the Rhode Island Secretary of State is:

104 CANTON STREET P.O. BOX 023028 PROVIDENCE , RI 02903-

The name of the registered agent as PRESENTLY shown in the corporate records on file with the Rhode Island Secretary of State is:

DOMINGO MOREL

SECTION III

The address of the NEW registered office is:

No. and Street: 61 DEWEY STREET
City or Town: PROVIDENCE   State: RI   Zip: 02909

The name of the NEW registered agent is: DORIS M. DE LOS SANTOS

SECTION IV

The address of the corporation's registered office and the address of the office of its registered agent, as changed, will be identical.

SECTION V

The change was authorized by resolution duly adopted by its board of directors.

Signed this 8 Day of July, 2010 at 7:12:48 AM. *This electronic signature of the individual or individuals signing this instrument constitutes the affirmation or acknowledgement of the signatory, under penalties of perjury, that this instrument is that individual's act and deed or the act and deed of the corporation, and that the facts stated herein are true, as of the date of the electronic filing, in compliance with R.I. Gen. Laws § 7-6.*

Rhode Island Latino Civic Fund
Corporate Name

By DORIS M. DE LOS SANTOS

    X Its President or   __ Its Vice President   (check one)

Form No. 641
Revised 09/07

© 2007 - 2010 State of Rhode Island and Providence Plantations
All Rights Reserved

RI SOS   Filing Number: 201064638770   Date: 07/08/2010 7:22 AM

State of Rhode Island and Providence Plantations
Office of the Secretary of State

Fee: $20.00

Division Of Business Services
148 W. River Street
Providence RI 02904-2615
(401) 222-3040

Non-Profit Corporation
Annual Report
Filing Period: June 1 - June 30

In accordance with R.I.G.L. 7-6-94, each corporation failing or refusing to file its annual report within the time prescribed by law (R.I.G.L. 7-6-91) is subject to a penalty fee of $25.00.

ANNUAL REPORT YEAR: 2010

1. **Corporate ID No.**   000125204

2. **Name of Corporation**   Rhode Island Latino Civic Fund

3. **State of Incorporation**
    State: RI

4. **Corporate Address in Rhode Island**

    No. and Street: PO BOX 23040
    City or Town: PROVIDENCE   State: RI   Zip: 02903   Country: USA

5. **Foreign Corporation. Enter Principal Office Address**

    No. and Street:
    City or Town: State: Zip: Country:

6. **Brief Description of the Character of the Affairs Which are Actually Conducted in Rhode Island**

    TO PROMOTE THE PARTICIPATION OF THE LATINO COMMUNITY IN THE CIVIC LIFE AND DEMOCRATIC PROCESSES OF RHODE ISLAND

7. **Names and Addresses of the Officers and Directors:**

    All officers and directors must be listed. If officers and/or directors have been elected, the title   Incorporator is no longer applicable; please delete

    THE NUMBER OF DIRECTORS OF A DOMESTIC(RHODE ISLAND)CORPORATION SHALL NOT BE LESS THAN THREE(3). R.I.G.L. 7-6-23

Title	Individual Name	Address
	First, Middle, Last, Suffix	Address, City or Town, State, Zip Code, Country
PRESIDENT	DORIS M. DE LOS SANTOS	61 DEWEY STREET PROVIDENCE, RI 02909 USA
SECRETARY	CARMEN DIAZ-JUSINO	80 BOWLET STREET PROVIDENCE, RI 02909 USA
VICE PRESIDENT	YSA LUNA	167 ROGER WILLIAMS AVENUE PROVIDENCE, RI 02907 USA
EXECUTIVE ASSISTANT	OBED PAPP	88 DEXTER ST PROVIDENCE, RI 02909 USA
DIRECTOR	BELKISS LUNA-SUAZO	230 ROGER WILLIAMS AVE. PROVIDENCE, R 02907 USA
DIRECTOR	MICHAEL NINA	299 PROMENADE PROVIDENCE, RI 02908 USA
DIRECTOR	DOMINGO MOREL	290 LEGION WAY CRANSTON, RI 02910 USA

8. REGISTERED AGENT IN RHODE ISLAND - DO NOT ALTER
Changes Require Filing of Form 641 - R.I.G.L. 7-6-13 / 7-6-78

DOMINGO MOREL 104 CANTON STREET P.O. BOX 023028 PROVIDENCE , RI 02903-

9. This report must be signed by either the President, Vice President, Secretary, Assistant Secretary, Treasurer, Receiver, or Trustee.

Signed this 8 Day of July, 2010 at 7:24:10 AM. *This electronic signature of the individual or individuals signing this instrument constitutes the affirmation or acknowledgement of the signatory, under penalties of perjury, that this instrument is that individual's act and deed or the act and deed of the corporation, and that the facts stated herein are true, as of the date of the electronic filing, in compliance with R.I. Gen. Laws § 7-6.*

By <u>DORIS M. DE LOS SANTOS</u>
Signature of Officer of the Corporation

    X President or   __ Vice President or   __ Secretary or   __ Assistant Secretary or

    __ Treasurer or   __ Receiver or   __ Trustee (check one)

This report cannot be accepted for filing if an officer has executed the form and he/she is not listed in Section 7.

Form No. 631
Revised 09/07

© 2007 - 2010 State of Rhode Island and Providence Plantations
All Rights Reserved

RI SOS   Filing Number: 201288831070   Date: 02/01/2012 11:05 AM

State of Rhode Island and Providence Plantations
Office of the Secretary of State

Fee: $20.00

Division Of Business Services
148 W. River Street
Providence RI 02904-2615
(401) 222-3040

Non-Profit Corporation
Annual Report
Filing Period: June 1 - June 30

In accordance with R.I.G.L. 7-6-94, each corporation failing or refusing to file its annual report within the time prescribed by law (R.I.G.L. 7-6-91) is subject to a penalty fee of $25.00.

ANNUAL REPORT YEAR: 2011

1. **Corporate ID No.**   000125204

2. **Name of Corporation**   Rhode Island Latino Civic Fund

3. **State of Incorporation**

   State: RI

4. **Corporate Address in Rhode Island**

   No. and Street: PO BOX 23040
   City or Town: PROVIDENCE   State: RI   Zip: 02903   Country: USA

5. **Foreign Corporation. Enter Principal Office Address**

   No. and Street:

   City or Town: State: Zip: Country:

6. **Brief Description of the Character of the Affairs Which are Actually Conducted in Rhode Island**

   TO PROMOTE THE PARTICIPATION OF THE LATINO COMMUNITY IN THE CIVIC LIFE AND DEMOCRATIC PROCESSES OF RHODE ISLAND

7. **Names and Addresses of the Officers and Directors:**

   All officers and directors must be listed. If officers and/or directors have been elected, the title   Incorporator is no longer applicable; please delete

   THE NUMBER OF DIRECTORS OF A DOMESTIC(RHODE ISLAND)CORPORATION SHALL NOT BE LESS THAN THREE(3). R.I.G.L. 7-6-23

Title	Individual Name	Address
	First, Middle, Last, Suffix	Address, City or Town, State, Zip Code, Country
EXECUTIVE ASSISTANT	OBED PAPP	88 DEXTER ST PROVIDENCE, RI 02909 USA
VICE PRESIDENT	CARMEN DIAZ-JUSINO	80 BOWLET STREET PROVIDENCE, RI 02909 USA
DIRECTOR	MICHAEL NINA	299 PROMENADE PROVIDENCE, RI 02908 USA
DIRECTOR	DORIS DE LOS SANTOS	61 DEWEY STREET PROVIDENCE, RI 02909 USA
DIRECTOR	TONY AFFIGNE	19 HOPE AVE. PROVIDENCE, RI 02906 USA
DIRECTOR	PAOLA FONSECA	50 VALLEY STREET PROVIDENCE, RI 02909 USA

8. REGISTERED AGENT IN RHODE ISLAND - DO NOT ALTER
Changes Require Filing of Form 641 - R.I.G.L. 7-6-13 / 7-6-78

DORIS M. DE LOS SANTOS 61 DEWEY STREET PROVIDENCE , RI 02909

9. This report must be signed by either the President, Vice President, Secretary, Assistant Secretary, Treasurer, Receiver, or Trustee.

Signed this 1 Day of February, 2012 at 11:05:53 AM. *This electronic signature of the individual or individuals signing this instrument constitutes the affirmation or acknowledgement of the signatory, under penalties of perjury, that this instrument is that individual's act and deed or the act and deed of the corporation, and that the facts stated herein are true, as of the date of the electronic filing, in compliance with R.I. Gen. Laws § 7-6.*

By DORIS M. DE LOS SANTOS
   Signature of Officer of the Corporation

   __ President or   __ Vice President or   __ Secretary or   __ Assistant Secretary or

   __ Treasurer or   __ Receiver or   **X** Trustee   (check one)

   This report cannot be accepted for filing if an officer has executed the form and he/she is not listed in Section 7.

Form No. 631
Revised 09/07

© 2007 - 2012 State of Rhode Island and Providence Plantations
All Rights Reserved

RI SOS Filing Number: 201295489370 Date: 07/31/2012 10:13 PM

State of Rhode Island and Providence Plantations
Office of the Secretary of State

Fee: $20.00

Division Of Business Services
148 W. River Street
Providence RI 02904-2615
(401) 222-3040

Non-Profit Corporation
Annual Report
Filing Period: June 1 - June 30

In accordance with R.I.G.L. 7-6-94, each corporation failing or refusing to file its annual report within the time prescribed by law (R.I.G.L. 7-6-91) is subject to a penalty fee of $25.00.

ANNUAL REPORT YEAR: 2012

1. Corporate ID No. 000125204

2. Name of Corporation Rhode Island Latino Civic Fund

3. State of Incorporation

State: RI

4. Corporate Address in Rhode Island

No. and Street: PO BOX 23040
City or Town: PROVIDENCE   State: RI   Zip: 02903 Country: USA

5. Foreign Corporation. Enter Principal Office Address

No. and Street:

City or Town: State: Zip: Country:

6. Brief Description of the Character of the Affairs Which are Actually Conducted in Rhode Island

TO PROMOTE THE PARTICIPATION OF THE LATINO COMMUNITY IN THE CIVIC LIFE AND DEMOCRATIC PROCESSES OF RHODE ISLAND

7. Names and Addresses of the Officers and Directors:

All officers and directors must be listed. If officers and/or directors have been elected, the title Incorporator is no longer applicable; please delete

THE NUMBER OF DIRECTORS OF A DOMESTIC(RHODE ISLAND)CORPORATION SHALL NOT BE LESS THAN THREE(3). R.I.G.L. 7-6-23

Title	Individual Name	Address
	First, Middle, Last, Suffix	Address, City or Town, State, Zip Code, Country
PRESIDENT	CARMEN DIAZ-JUSINO	80 BOWLETT STREET PROVIDENCE, RI 02909 USA
TREASURER	BETTY BERNAL	27 CUMERFORD PROVIDENCE, RI 02909 USA
SECRETARY	MELIDA ESPINAL	37 LONGFELLOW TERRACE PROVIDENCE, RI 02907 USA
VICE PRESIDENT	ANNA CANO-MORALES	23 REDWOOD DR. NORTH PROVIDENCE, RI 02911 USA
EXECUTIVE ASSISTANT	OBED PAPP	88 DEXTER ST PROVIDENCE, RI 02909 USA
DIRECTOR	DORIS DE LOS SANTOS	61 DEWEY STREET PROVIDENCE, RI 02909 USA
DIRECTOR	TONY AFFIGNE	19 HOPE AVE. PROVIDENCE, RI 02906 USA
DIRECTOR	PAOLA FONSECA	50 VALLEY STREET PROVIDENCE, RI 02909 USA
DIRECTOR	PAOLA FONSECA	

8. REGISTERED AGENT IN RHODE ISLAND - DO NOT ALTER
Changes Require Filing of Form 641 - R.I.G.L. 7-6-13 / 7-6-78

DORIS M. DE LOS SANTOS 61 DEWEY STREET PROVIDENCE , RI 02909

9. This report must be signed by either the President, Vice President, Secretary, Assistant Secretary, Treasurer, Receiver, or Trustee.

Signed this 31 Day of July, 2012 at 10:23:08 PM. *This electronic signature of the individual or individuals signing this instrument constitutes the affirmation or acknowledgement of the signatory, under penalties of perjury, that this instrument is that individual's act and deed or the act and deed of the corporation, and that the facts stated herein are true, as of the date of the electronic filing, in compliance with R.I. Gen. Laws § 7-6.*

By CARMEN DIAZ-JUSINO
   Signature of Officer of the Corporation

   X President or __ Vice President or __ Secretary or __ Assistant Secretary or

   __ Treasurer or __ Receiver or __ Trustee (check one)

   This report cannot be accepted for filing if an officer has executed the form and he/she is not listed in Section 7.

Form No. 631
Revised 09/07

© 2007 - 2012 State of Rhode Island and Providence Plantations
All Rights Reserved

State of Rhode Island and Providence Plantations
Office of the Secretary of State

Fee: $10.00

Division Of Business Services
148 W. River Street
Providence RI 02904-2615
(401) 222-3040

Non-Profit Corporation
Statement of Change of Registered Agent by the Corporation
(Section 7-6-78 of the General Laws of Rhode Island, 1956, as amended)

SECTION I

The name of the corporation is Rhode Island Latino Civic Fund

SECTION II

The address of the registered office as PRESENTLY shown in the corporate records on file with the Rhode Island Secretary of State is:

61 DEWEY STREET PROVIDENCE , RI 02909

The name of the registered agent as PRESENTLY shown in the corporate records on file with the Rhode Island Secretary of State is:

DORIS M. DE LOS SANTOS

SECTION III

The address of the NEW registered office is:

No. and Street: 80 BOWLETT STREET
City or Town: PROVIDENCE   State: RI   Zip: 02909

The name of the NEW registered agent is: CARMEN DIAZ-JUSINO

SECTION IV

The address of the corporation's registered office and the address of the office of its registered agent, as changed, will be identical.

SECTION V

The change was authorized by resolution duly adopted by its board of directors.

Signed this **31 Day of July, 2012 at 10:34:30 PM.** *This electronic signature of the individual or individuals signing this instrument constitutes the affirmation or acknowledgement of the signatory, under penalties of perjury, that this instrument is that individual's act and deed or the act and deed of the corporation, and that the facts stated herein are true, as of the date of the electronic filing, in compliance with R.I. Gen. Laws § 7-6.*

Rhode Island Latino Civic Fund
Corporate Name

By CARMEN DIAZ-JUSINO

  X Its President or __ Its Vice President   (check one)

Form No. 641
Revised 09/07

© 2007 - 2012 State of Rhode Island and Providence Plantations
All Rights Reserved

RI SOS   Filing Number: 201321609880   Date: 05/27/2013 9:51 PM

State of Rhode Island and Providence Plantations
Office of the Secretary of State

Fee: $10.00

Division Of Business Services
148 W. River Street
Providence RI 02904-2615
(401) 222-3040

Non-Profit Corporation
Statement of Change of Registered Agent by the Corporation
(Section 7-6-78 of the General Laws of Rhode Island, 1956, as amended)

SECTION I

The name of the corporation is   Rhode Island Latino Civic Fund

SECTION II

The address of the registered office as PRESENTLY shown in the corporate records on file with the Rhode Island Secretary of State is:

80 BOWLETT STREET   PROVIDENCE , RI 02909

The name of the registered agent as PRESENTLY shown in the corporate records on file with the Rhode Island Secretary of State is:

CARMEN DIAZ-JUSINO

SECTION III

The address of the NEW registered office is:

No. and Street: 101 HILLCREST DRIVE
City or Town: CRANSTON   State: RI   Zip: 02921

The name of the NEW registered agent is: GONZALO CUERVO

SECTION IV

The address of the corporation's registered office and the address of the office of its registered agent, as changed, will be identical.

SECTION V

The change was authorized by resolution duly adopted by its board of directors.

Signed this 27 Day of May, 2013 at 9:55:09 PM. *This electronic signature of the individual or individuals signing this instrument constitutes the affirmation or acknowledgement of the signatory, under penalties of perjury, that this instrument is that individual's act and deed or the act and deed of the corporation, and that the facts stated herein are true, as of the date of the electronic filing, in compliance with R.I. Gen. Laws § 7-6.*

Rhode Island Latino Civic Fund
Corporate Name

By GONZALO CUERVO

   X Its President or   __ Its Vice President   (check one)

Form No. 641
Revised 09/07

© 2007 - 2013 State of Rhode Island and Providence Plantations
All Rights Reserved

RI SOS   Filing Number: 201438098250   Date: 04/08/2014 4:26 PM

STATE OF RHODE ISLAND AND PROVIDENCE PLANTATIONS
Office of the Secretary of State - Division of Business Services
148 W. River Street, Providence, Rhode Island 02904-2615
Phone: (401) 222-3040 ~ Email: corporations@sos.ri.gov ~ Website: www.sos.ri.gov/business

NON-PROFIT CORPORATION ANNUAL REPORT FOR THE YEAR 2013

Filing Period: June 1 - June 30 · This report must be typed or printed legibly.
Filing Fee: $20.00 · FAILURE TO FILE THIS REPORT BY JULY 30 WILL RESULT IN A $25.00 PENALTY FEE.

1. Entity ID No.	2. Exact name of the Corporation
125204	Rhode Island Latino Civic Fund
3. State of Incorporation	4. Brief description of the character of business conducted in Rhode Island
RI	To promote civic participation and democratic engagement within Rhode Island's Latino Co...

5. Principal office address	City	State	Zip
101 Hillcrest Drive	Cranston	RI	02921

6. LIST ALL OFFICERS (NAMES AND ADDRESSES) ("X" BOX FOR ATTACHMENT)

President Name	Vice-President Name
Gonzalo Cuervo	Jose F. Batista
Street Address: 101 Hillcrest Drive	Street Address: 133 Byfield Street
City: Cranston State: RI Zip: 02921	City: Providence State: RI Zip: 02905
Secretary Name	Treasurer Name
Ingrid Arcaya	Melba Depeña
Street Address: 11 North Avenue	Street Address: 117 Dora Street
City: Providence State: RI Zip: 02906	City: Providence State: RI Zip: 02906

7. LIST ALL DIRECTORS (NAMES AND ADDRESSES). RHODE ISLAND CORPORATIONS MUST LIST NO LESS THAN THREE (3) DIRECTORS

Director Name	Director Name
Melida Espinal	Doris Blanchard
Street Address: 37 Longfellow Terrace	Street Address: One Chestnut Street
City: Providence State: RI Zip: 02907	City: Providence State: RI Zip: 02903
Director Name	Director Name
Betty Bernal	Tony Affigne
Street Address: 27 Comerford St.	Street Address: 117 Dora Street
City: Providence State: RI Zip: 02909	City: Providence State: RI Zip: 02906

8. REGISTERED AGENT IN RHODE ISLAND
This information is currently of record in the Office of the Secretary of State. Changes require filing Form 641.

This report must be signed by either the President, Vice-President, Secretary, Assistant Secretary, Treasurer, Receiver or Trustee

FILED
APR 08 2014
49-22187

Under penalty of perjury, I declare and affirm that I have examined this report, including any accompanying schedules and statements, and that all statements contained herein are true and correct.

Signature of Officer: Gonzalo Cuervo
Print or Type Name of Officer: Gonzalo Cuervo
Title of Officer: President

A.A. 4:26 pm

Form No. 631   105441-2-903102
Revised: 05/2012

RI Latino Civic Fund officers (continued)

9) Claudia Cardona
   365 Post Road
   East Greenwich, RI 02818

10) Jackie Alvarez
    301 Reservoir Avenue
    Providence, RI 02907

11) Obed Papp
    17 Dexter Street
    Providence, RI 02908

Not Secure — business.sos.ri.gov

Phone: (401) 222-3040 ~ Email: corporations@sos.ri.gov ~ Website: www.sos.ri.gov

NON-PROFIT CORPORATION ANNUAL REPORT FOR THE YEAR 2014

Filing Period: June 1 - June 30 · This report must be typed or printed legibly.
Filing Fee: $20.00 · FAILURE TO FILE THIS REPORT BY JULY 30 WILL RESULT IN A $25.00 PENALTY FEE.

1. Entity ID No.	2. Exact name of the Corporation			
125204	Rhode Island Latino Civic Fund			
3. State of Incorporation	4. Corporate Address in RI - Street Address		City	Zip
RI	133 Byfield Street		Providence	02905
5. Foreign corporation. Enter principal office address		City	State	Zip

6. Brief description of the character of business conducted in Rhode Island
To promote civic participation and democratic engagement within Rhode Island's Latino community

7. LIST ALL OFFICERS (NAMES AND ADDRESSES) ("X" BOX FOR ATTACHMENT) ☐

President Name	Jose F. Batista	Vice-President Name	Melida Espinal
Street Address	133 Byfield Street	Street Address	37 Longfellow Terrace
City Providence	State RI Zip 02905	City Providence	State RI Zip 02907
Secretary Name	Melida Espinal	Treasurer Name	Travis Escobar
Street Address	37 Longfellow Terrace	Street Address	167 Webster Avenue
City Providence	State RI Zip 02907	City Providence	State RI Zip 02909

8. LIST ALL DIRECTORS (NAMES AND ADDRESSES). RHODE ISLAND CORPORATIONS **MUST** LIST NO LESS THAN THREE (3) DIRECTORS ("X" BOX FOR ATTACHMENT) ☒

Director Name	Gonzalo Cuervo	Director Name	Doris Blanchard
Street Address	101 Hillcrest Drive	Street Address	1 Chestnut Street
City Cranston	State RI Zip 02921	City Providence	State RI Zip 02903
Director Name	Mercedes Betty Bernal	Director Name	Tony Affigne
Street Address	27 Comerford Street	Street Address	117 Dora Street
City Providence	State RI Zip 02909	City Providence	State RI Zip 02906

9. REGISTERED AGENT IN RHODE ISLAND
This information is currently of record in the Office of the Secretary of State. Changes require filing Form 641.

This report must be signed by either the President, Vice-President, Secretary, Assistant Secretary, Treasurer, Receiver or Trustee

FILED
JUN 11 2014

Under penalty of perjury, I declare and affirm that I have examined this report, including any accompanying schedules and statements, and that all statements contained herein are true and correct.

Signature of Officer: [signed] 6/11/14
Print or Type Name of Officer: Jose F. Batista
Title of Officer: President

Form No. 631

Directors (continued)

Ingrid Ardaya
11 North Avenue
Providence, RI 02906

Obed Papp
117 Dexter Street
Providence, RI 02908

Jackie Alvarez
301 Reservoir Avenue
Providence, RI 02907

Melba Depeña
117 Dora Street
Providence, RI 02906

Claudia Cardona
4365 Post Road
East Greenwich, RI 02818

State of Rhode Island and Providence Plantations
Office of the Secretary of State

Fee: $10.00

Division Of Business Services
148 W. River Street
Providence RI 02904-2615
(401) 222-3040

Non-Profit Corporation
Statement of Change of Registered Agent by the Corporation
(Section 7-6-78 of the General Laws of Rhode Island, 1956, as amended)

SECTION I

The name of the corporation is Rhode Island Latino Civic Fund

SECTION II

The address of the registered office as PRESENTLY shown in the corporate records on file with the Rhode Island Secretary of State is:

101 HILLCREST DRIVE CRANSTON , RI 02921

The name of the registered agent as PRESENTLY shown in the corporate records on file with the Rhode Island Secretary of State is:

GONZALO CUERVO

SECTION III

The address of the NEW registered office is:

No. and Street:	133 BYFIELD STREET			
City or Town:	PROVIDENCE	State: RI	Zip:	02905

The name of the NEW registered agent is: JOSE F. BATISTA

SECTION IV

The address of the corporation's registered office and the address of the office of its registered agent, as changed, will be identical.

SECTION V

The change was authorized by resolution duly adopted by its board of directors.

Signed this 1 Day of May, 2015 at 7:55:55 AM. *This electronic signature of the individual or individuals signing this instrument constitutes the affirmation or acknowledgement of the signatory, under penalties of perjury, that this instrument is that individual's act and deed or the act and deed of the corporation, and that the facts stated herein are true, as of the date of the electronic filing, in compliance with R.I. Gen. Laws § 7-6.*

Rhode Island Latino Civic Fund
Corporate Name

By JOSE F. BATISTA

  X Its President or   __ Its Vice President   (check one)

Form No. 641
Revised 09/07

© 2007 - 2015 State of Rhode Island and Providence Plantations
All Rights Reserved

RI SOS   Filing Number: 201608686670   Date: 09/12/2016 1:49 PM

State of Rhode Island and Providence Plantations
Department of State - Business Services Division

Annual Report for the year: 2015
Non-Profit Corporation
- Filing period: June 1 - June 30
- Filing Fee: $20.00
- Penalty: Additional $25.00 fee if form is not filed by July 30.

RECEIVED
SECRETARY OF STATE
CORPORATIONS DIV
2016 SEP 12 PM 1:48

1. **Entity ID Number:** 125204
2. **Exact name of the Corporation:** Rhode Island Latino Civic Fund
3. **State of Incorporation:** RI
4. **Brief description of the character of business conducted in Rhode Island:** To promote Civic participation + engagement within Latino community
5. **Principal Office Address:** PO Box 2324, Providence, RI 02903
6. **List ALL officers (names and addresses):**

- **President Name:** Jose F. Batista
  - Street Address: 123 Byfield Street
  - City: Providence, State: RI, Zip: 02905
- **Vice-President Name:** Melida Espinal
  - Street Address: 37 Longfellow Terrace
  - City: Providence, State: RI, Zip: 02907
- **Secretary Name:** Obed Papp
  - Street Address: 117 Dexter Street
  - City: Providence, State: RI, Zip: 02908
- **Treasurer Name:** Sylvia Bernal
  - Street Address: 26 Vernon Street
  - City: Providence, State: RI, Zip: 02903

7. **List ALL directors (names and addresses). RI Corporations MUST list at least THREE directors.**

- **Director Name:** Doris Blanchard
  - Street Address: 1 Chestnut Street
  - City: Providence, State: RI, Zip: 00903
- **Director Name:** Jackie Alvarez
  - Street Address: 301 Reservoir Ave
  - City: Providence, State: RI, Zip: 02907
- **Director Name:** Mercedes Betty Bernal
  - Street Address: 27 Comerford Street
  - City: Providence, State: RI, Zip: 02909

8. **Registered Agent in Rhode Island.** This information is currently of record in the Department of State. Changes require filing Form 641.

Under penalty of perjury, I declare and affirm that I have examined this report, including any accompanying schedules and statements, and that all statements contained herein are true and correct.

Name of Officer/Authorized Representative: Jose F. Batista
Date: 9/12/2016
Signature of Officer/Authorized Representative: [signed]

FILED 1:49
SEP 12 2016
By C 11948562

MAIL TO:
Division of Business Services
148 W. River Street, Providence, Rhode Island 02904-2615
Phone: (401) 222-3040

FORM 631 - Revised: 05/2016

RI SOS Filing Number: 201608686300 Date: 09/12/2016 1:50 PM

State of Rhode Island and Providence Plantations
Department of State - Business Services Division

Annual Report for the year: 2016
Non-Profit Corporation
→ Filing period: June 1 - June 30
→ Filing Fee: $20.00
→ Penalty: Additional $25.00 fee if form is not filed by July 30.

RECEIVED
SECRETARY OF STATE
CORPORATIONS DIV
2016 SEP 12 PM 1:48

1. Entity ID Number	2. Exact name of the Corporation
125204	Rhode Island Latino Civic Fund

3. State of Incorporation	4. Brief description of the character of business conducted in Rhode Island
RI	To promote civic participation + engagement within Latino communi...

5. Principal Office Address	City	State	Zip
PO BOX 23124	Providence	RI	02903

6. List ALL officers (names and addresses)

President Name: Jose F. Batista	Vice-President Name: Melida Espinal
Street Address: 133 Boyfield Street	Street Address: 37 Longfellow Terrace
City: Providence State: RI Zip: 02905	City: Providence State: RI Zip: 02907
Secretary Name: Obed Papp	Treasurer Name: Sylvia Bernal
Street Address: 117 Dexter Street	Street Address: 26 Vernon Street
City: Providence State: RI Zip: 02908	City: Providence State: RI Zip: 02903

7. List ALL directors (names and addresses). RI Corporations MUST list at least THREE directors.

Director Name: Doris Blanchard	Director Name: Jackie Alvarez
Street Address: 1 Chestnut Street	Street Address: 301 Reservoir Avenue
City: Providence State: RI Zip: 00903	City: Providence State: RI Zip: 02907
Director Name: Mercedes Betty Bernal	Director Name:
Street Address: 27 Comerford Street	Street Address:
City: Providence State: RI Zip: 02909	City: State: Zip:

8. Registered Agent in Rhode Island. This information is currently of record in the Department of State. Changes require filing Form 641.

Under penalty of perjury, I declare and affirm that I have examined this report, including any accompanying schedules and statements, and that all statements contained herein are true and correct.

Name of Officer/Authorized Representative: Jose F. Batista
Date: 9/12/2016

FILED 1:50
SEP 12 2016
By LC 1194852

MAIL TO:
Division of Business Services
148 W. River Street, Providence, Rhode Island 02904-2615
Phone: (401) 222-3040

FORM 631 - Revised: 05/2016

RI SOS Filing Number: 201866638220 Date: 5/22/2018 10:49:00 AM

State of Rhode Island and Providence Plantations
Department of State - Business Services Division

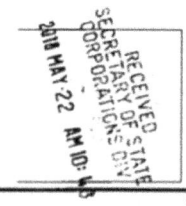

Annual Report for the year: 2017
Non-Profit Corporation
→ Filing period: June 1 - June 30
→ Filing Fee: $20.00
→ Penalty: Additional $25.00 fee if form is not filed by July 30.

1. Entity ID Number	2. Exact name of the Corporation
125204	RHODE ISLAND LATINO CIVIC FUND

3. State of Incorporation	5. Brief description of the character of business conducted in Rhode Island
RI	TO PROMOTE CIVIC PARTICIPATION AND ENGAGEMENT WITHIN LATINO COMMUNITY

4. NAICS Code
813990

6. Principal Office Address	City	State	Zip
127 DORRANCE STREET, 4TH FLOOR	PROVIDENCE	RI	02903

7. List ALL officers (names and addresses)

President Name: JOSEPH B. MOLINA FLYNN			Vice-President Name: MARCELA BETANCUR		
Street Address: 127 DORRANCE STREET, 4TH FLOOR			Street Address: 28 MAY STREET		
City: PROVIDENCE	State: RI	Zip: 02903	City: NORTH PROVIDENCE	State: RI	Zip: 02904
Secretary Name: Patricia Socarras			Treasurer Name: WESLEY RODAS		
Street Address: 144 Parkview Drive, Apt. 35			Street Address: 136 CHANDLER AVE		
City: Pawtucket	State: RI	Zip: 02861	City: PAWTUCKET	State: RI	Zip: 02860

8. List ALL directors (names and addresses) RI Corporations MUST list at least THREE directors

Director Name: Sol Taubin			Director Name: LUANNE SANTELISES		
Street Address: 29 WINFIELD ROAD			Street Address: 222 RESERVOIR AVENUE		
City: PROVIDENCE	State: RI	Zip: 02906	City: PROVIDENCE	State: RI	Zip: 02907
Director Name: DIANA PERDOMO			Director Name:		
Street Address: 1565 Main Road			Street Address:		
City: TIVERTON	State: RI	Zip: 02878	City:	State:	Zip:

9. Registered Agent in Rhode Island. This information is currently of record in the Department of State. Changes require filing Form 641

Under penalty of perjury, I declare and affirm that I have examined this report, including any accompanying schedules and statements, and that all statements contained herein are true and correct.

Name of Officer/Authorized Representative: **JOSEPH B. MOLINA FLYNN**
Date: 5/22/18

Signature of Officer/Authorized Representative

FILED MAY 22 2018 10:49
BY 2554428

MAIL TO:
Division of Business Services
148 W. River Street, Providence, Rhode Island 02904-2615
Phone: (401) 222-3040
Website: www.sos.ri.gov

FORM 631 - Revised: 11/2017

RI SOS Filing Number: 201866637700   Date: 5/22/2018 10:50:00 AM

State of Rhode Island and Providence Plantations
Department of State - Business Services Division

Annual Report for the year: 2018
Non-Profit Corporation
→ Filing period: June 1 - June 30
→ Filing Fee: $20.00
→ Penalty: Additional $25.00 fee if form is not filed by July 30.

RECEIVED 2018 MAY 22 AM 10:4 SECRETARY OF STATE CORPORATIONS DIV

1. Entity ID Number	2. Exact name of the Corporation
125204	**RHODE ISLAND LATINO CIVIC FUND**

3. State of Incorporation	5. Brief description of the character of business conducted in Rhode Island
RI	TO PROMOTE CIVIC PARTICIPATION AND ENGAGEMENT WITHIN LATINO COMMUNITY

4. NAICS Code 813990

6. Principal Office Address	City	State	Zip
127 DORRANCE STREET, 4TH FLOOR	PROVIDENCE	RI	02903

7. List ALL officers (names and addresses) Check the box to indicate an attachment ☐

President Name JOSEPH MOLINA FLYNN				Vice-President Name MARCELA BETANCUR			
Street Address 127 DORRANCE STREET, 4TH FLOOR				Street Address 28 MAY STREET			
City PROVIDENCE	State RI	Zip 02903		City NORTH PROVIDENCE	State RI	Zip 02904	
Secretary Name Patricia Socarras				Treasurer Name WESLEY RODAS			
Street Address 144 Parkview Drive, Apt. 35				Street Address 136 CHANDLER AVE			
City Pawtucket	State RI	Zip 02861		City PAWTUCKET	State RI	Zip 02860

8. List ALL directors (names and addresses). RI Corporations MUST list at least THREE directors. Check the box to indicate an attachment ☐

Director Name Sol Taubin				Director Name LUANNE SANTELISES			
Street Address 29 WINFIELD ROAD				Street Address 222 RESERVOIR AVENUE			
City PROVIDENCE	State RI	Zip 02906		City PROVIDENCE	State RI	Zip 02907	
Director Name DIANA PERDOMO				Director Name			
Street Address 1565 Main Road				Street Address			
City TIVERTON	State RI	Zip 02878		City	State	Zip	

9. Registered Agent in Rhode Island. This information is currently of record in the Department of State. Changes require filing Form 641.

Under penalty of perjury, I declare and affirm that I have examined this report, including any accompanying schedules and statements, and that all statements contained herein are true and correct.

This report must be signed by either the President, Vice President, Secretary, Assistant Secretary, Treasurer, duly Authorized Representative, Receiver or Trustee.

Name of Officer/Authorized Representative	Date
JOSEPH D MOLINA FLYNN	FILED 5/22/18

Signature of Officer/Authorized Representative

SIGN DOCUMENT HERE   MAY 22 2018

BY 25544218 10:50

MAIL TO:
Division of Business Services
148 W. River Street, Providence, Rhode Island 02904-2615
Phone: (401) 222-3040
Website: www.sos.ri.gov

FORM 631 - Revised: 11/2017

RI SOS Filing Number: 201866635490   Date: 5/22/2018 10:51:00 AM

State of Rhode Island and Providence Plantations
Department of State - Business Services Division

Statement of Change of Agent
DOMESTIC or FOREIGN Non-Profit Corporation

→ Filing Fee: $10.00

Pursuant to the provisions of RIGL 7-6-13 or 7-6-78 the undersigned corporation submits the following statement for the purpose of changing its registered agent in the State of Rhode Island:

1. Entity ID Number	2. Exact Name of the Corporation
000125204	Rhode Island Latino Civic Fund

3. The address of the registered office as PRESENTLY shown in the records on file with the RI Department of State:

Street Address: 133 BYFIELD STREET

City/Town	State	Zip
PROVIDENCE	RHODE ISLAND	02905

4. The name of the registered agent as PRESENTLY shown in the records on file with the RI Department of State:

JOSE F. BATISTA

5. The address of the NEW registered office is:

Street Address (NOT a P.O. Box): 127 Dorrance Street, 4th Floor

City/Town	State	Zip
PROVIDENCE	RHODE ISLAND	02903

6. The name of the NEW registered agent is:

JOSEPH MOLINA FLYNN

7. The address of the corporation's registered office and the address of the office of its registered agent, as changed, will be identical.

8. The change was authorized by a resolution duly adopted by its board of directors.

Under penalty of perjury, I declare and affirm that I have examined this Statement of Change of Registered Agent by the Corporation, and that all statements contained herein are true and correct.

Name of President/Vice President of the Corporation	Date
JOSEPH MOLINA FLYNN	5/22/2018

Signature of President/Vice President of the Corporation

FILED
MAY 22 2018 S 10:51
BY 25544218

MAIL TO:
Division of Business Services
148 W. River Street, Providence, Rhode Island 02904-2615
Phone: (401) 222-3040
Website: www.sos.ri.gov

FORM 641 - Revised 07/2016

State of Rhode Island and Providence Plantations
Office of the Secretary of State

Fee: $20.00

Division Of Business Services
148 W. River Street
Providence RI 02904-2615
(401) 222-3040

Non-Profit Corporation
Annual Report
Filing Period: June 1 - June 30

In accordance with R.I.G.L. 7-6-94, each corporation failing or refusing to file its annual report within the time prescribed by law (R.I.G.L. 7-6-91) is subject to a penalty fee of $25.00.

ANNUAL REPORT YEAR: 2019

1. Corporate ID No. 000125204

2. Name of Corporation RHODE ISLAND LATINO CIVIC FUND

3. State of Incorporation

State: RI

ARTICLE III

Using the dropdown labeled NAICS Code below, select the classification title that describes the primary type of activity in which your entity engages. The box to the right of the dropdown will populate a NAICS Code based on the chosen selection. If the NAICS Code is known, enter it into the box on the right. For further assistance with selecting a classification click here.

NAICS Code | 6
813990

4. Corporate Address in Rhode Island

No. and Street: 127 DORRANCE STREET, 4TH FLOOR
City or Town: PROVIDENCE   State: RI   Zip: 02903   Country: USA

5. Foreign Corporation. Enter Principal Office Address

No. and Street:

City or Town: State: Zip: Country:

6. Brief Description of the Character of the Affairs Which are Actually Conducted in Rhode Island

TO PROMOTE THE PARTICIPATION OF THE LATINO COMMUNITY IN THE CIVIC LIFE AND DEMOCRATIC PROCESSES OF RHODE ISLAND

7. Names and Addresses of the Officers and Directors:

All officers and directors must be listed. If officers and/or directors have been elected, the title Incorporator is no longer applicable; please delete

THE NUMBER OF DIRECTORS OF A DOMESTIC(RHODE ISLAND)CORPORATION SHALL NOT BE LESS THAN THREE(3). R.I.G.L. 7-6-23

Title	Individual Name First, Middle, Last, Suffix	Address Address, City or Town, State, Zip Code, Country
PRESIDENT	JOSEPH MOLINA FLYNN	127 DORRANCE STREET, 4TH FLOOR PROVIDENCE, RI 02903 USA
TREASURER	WESLEY RODAS	136 CHANDLER AVENUE PAWTUCKET, RI 02860 USA
SECRETARY	PATRICIA SOCARRAS	144 PARKVIEW DR APT 35 PAWTUCKET, RI 02861 USA
VICE PRESIDENT	MARCELA BETANCUR	28 MAY STREET NORTH PROVIDENCE, RI 02904 USA
DIRECTOR	DIANA PERDOMO	1565 MAIN ROAD TIVERTON, RI 02878 USA
DIRECTOR	LUANNE SANTELISES	222 RESERVOIR AVE PROVIDENCE, RI 02907 USA

8. REGISTERED AGENT IN RHODE ISLAND - DO NOT ALTER
Changes Require Filing of Form 641 - R.I.G.L. 7-6-13 / 7-6-78

JOSEPH MOLINA FLYNN   127 DORRANCE STREET, 4TH FLOOR   PROVIDENCE, RI 02903

9. This report must be signed by either the President, Vice President, Secretary, Assistant Secretary, Treasurer, duly Authorized Representative, Receiver, or Trustee.

Signed this 25 Day of July, 2019 at 5:26:14 PM by the authorized person. *This electronic signature of the individual or individuals signing this instrument constitutes the affirmation or acknowledgement of the signatory, under penalties of perjury, that this instrument is that individual's act and deed or the act and deed of the company, and that the facts stated herein are true, as of the date of the electronic filing, in compliance with R.I. Gen. Laws § 7-6.*

By   JOSEPH MOLINA FLYNN
Signature of Authorized Person

Form No. 631
Revised 09/07

© 2007 - 2019 State of Rhode Island and Providence Plantations
All Rights Reserved

RI SOS   Filing Number: 202043888160   Date: 7/1/2020 7:12:00 PM

State of Rhode Island and Providence Plantations
Office of the Secretary of State

Division Of Business Services
148 W. River Street
Providence RI 02904-2615
(401) 222-3040

Fee: $20.00

Non-Profit Corporation
Annual Report
Filing Period: June 1 - June 30

In accordance with R.I.G.L. 7-6-94, each corporation failing or refusing to file its annual report within the time prescribed by law (R.I.G.L. 7-6-91) is subject to a penalty fee of $25.00.

ANNUAL REPORT YEAR: 2020

1. Corporate ID No.   000125204

2. Name of Corporation   RHODE ISLAND LATINO CIVIC FUND

3. State of Incorporation

State: RI

ARTICLE III

Using the dropdown labeled NAICS Code below, select the classification title that describes the primary type of activity in which your entity engages. The box to the right of the dropdown will populate a NAICS Code based on the chosen selection. If the NAICS Code is known, enter it into the box on the right. For further assistance with selecting a classification click here.

NAICS Code
813990

4. Corporate Address in Rhode Island

No. and Street: 127 DORRANCE STREET, 4TH FLOOR
City or Town: PROVIDENCE   State: RI   Zip: 02903   Country: USA

5. Foreign Corporation. Enter Principal Office Address

No. and Street:

City or Town: State: Zip: Country:

6. Brief Description of the Character of the Affairs Which are Actually Conducted in Rhode Island

TO PROMOTE THE PARTICIPATION OF THE LATINO COMMUNITY IN THE CIVIC LIFE AND DEMOCRATIC PROCESSES OF RHODE ISLAND

7. Names and Addresses of the Officers and Directors:

All officers and directors must be listed. If officers and/or directors have been elected, the title Incorporator is no longer applicable; please delete

THE NUMBER OF DIRECTORS OF A DOMESTIC(RHODE ISLAND)CORPORATION SHALL NOT BE LESS THAN THREE(3). R.I.G.L. 7-6-23

Title	Individual Name First, Middle, Last, Suffix	Address Address, City or Town, State, Zip Code, Country
PRESIDENT	JOSEPH MOLINA FLYNN	127 DORRANCE STREET, 4TH FLOOR PROVIDENCE, RI 02903 USA
SECRETARY	PATRICIA SOCARRAS	144 PARKVIEW DR APT 35 PAWTUCKET, RI 02861 USA
VICE PRESIDENT	MARCELA BETANCUR	28 MAY STREET NORTH PROVIDENCE, RI 02904 USA
DIRECTOR	DIANA PERDOMO	1565 MAIN ROAD TIVERTON, RI 02878 USA
DIRECTOR	LUANNE SANTELISES	222 RESERVOIR AVE PROVIDENCE, RI 02907 USA
DIRECTOR	DIONY GARCIA	176 ATLANTIC AVE. UNIT 2 PROVIDENCE, RI 02907 USA

8. REGISTERED AGENT IN RHODE ISLAND - DO NOT ALTER
Changes Require Filing of Form 641 - R.I.G.L. 7-6-13 / 7-6-78

JOSEPH MOLINA FLYNN 127 DORRANCE STREET, 4TH FLOOR PROVIDENCE , RI 02903

9. This report must be signed by either the President, Vice President, Secretary, Assistant Secretary, Treasurer, duly Authorized Representative, Receiver, or Trustee.

Signed this 1 Day of July, 2020 at 7:13:32 PM by the authorized person. *This electronic signature of the individual or individuals signing this instrument constitutes the affirmation or acknowledgement of the signatory, under penalties of perjury, that this instrument is that individual's act and deed or the act and deed of the company, and that the facts stated herein are true, as of the date of the electronic filing, in compliance with R.I. Gen. Laws § 7-6.*

By JOSEPH MOLINA FLYNN
    Signature of Authorized Person

Form No. 631
Revised 09/07

© 2007 - 2020 State of Rhode Island and Providence Plantations
All Rights Reserved

RI SOS Filing Number: 202198883470 Date: 6/30/2021 10:36:00 PM

State of Rhode Island
Office of the Secretary of State

Fee: $20.00

Division Of Business Services
148 W. River Street
Providence RI 02904-2615
(401) 222-3040

Non-Profit Corporation
Annual Report
Filing Period: June 1 - June 30

In accordance with R.I.G.L. 7-6-94, each corporation failing or refusing to file its annual report within the time prescribed by law (R.I.G.L. 7-6-91) is subject to a penalty fee of $25.00.

ANNUAL REPORT YEAR: 2021

1. Corporate ID No. 000125204

2. Name of Corporation RHODE ISLAND LATINO CIVIC FUND

3. State of Incorporation

State: RI

ARTICLE III

Using the dropdown labeled NAICS Code below, select the classification title that describes the primary type of activity in which your entity engages. The box to the right of the dropdown will populate a NAICS Code based on the chosen selection. If the NAICS Code is known, enter it into the box on the right. For further assistance with selecting a classification click here.

NAICS Code
813990

4. Principal Office Address

No. and Street: 26 VERNON ST
City or Town: PROVIDENCE   State: RI   Zip: 02903   Country: USA

5. Foreign Corporation. Enter Principal Office Address

No. and Street:

City or Town: State: Zip: Country:

5. Brief Description of the Character of the Affairs Conducted in Rhode Island

TO PROMOTE THE PARTICIPATION OF THE LATINO COMMUNITY IN THE CIVIC LIFE AND DEMOCRATIC PROCESSES OF RHODE ISLAND

6. Names and Addresses of the Officers and Directors:

All Directors and Officers must be listed individually. The number of DIRECTORS of a Rhode Island Corporation shall not be less than 3.

Title	Individual Name	Address
	First, Middle, Last, Suffix	Address, City or Town, State, Zip Code, Country
PRESIDENT	MELITZI TORRES	19 CUTE ST PAWTUCKET, RI 02860 USA
TREASURER	SYLVIA BERNAL	26 VERNONST PROVIDENCE, RI 02903 USA
VICE PRESIDENT	MARIBEL ECHEVERRY	87 VARNUM AVE PAWTUCKET, RI 02860 USA
DIRECTOR	VICTOR REGINO	56 BLISS EAST PROVIDENCE, RI 02914 USA
DIRECTOR	MARIA CRUZ	90 SAGE DR WARWICK, RI 02886 USA
DIRECTOR	KATYA M RODRIGUEZ ROMAN	63 PITMAN UNIT 3 PROVIDENCE, RI 02906 USA

7. REGISTERED AGENT IN RHODE ISLAND - DO NOT ALTER
Changes Require Filing of Form 641 - R.I.G.L. 7-6-13 / 7-6-78

SYLVIA BERNAL   26 VERNON ST   PROVIDENCE , RI   02903

8. This report must be signed by either the President, Vice President, Secretary, Assistant Secretary, Treasurer, duly Authorized Representative, Receiver, or Trustee.

Signed this 30 Day of June, 2021 at 10:39:52 PM by the authorized person. *This electronic signature of the individual or individuals signing this instrument constitutes the affirmation or acknowledgement of the signatory, under penalties of perjury, that this instrument is that individual's act and deed or the act and deed of the company, and that the facts stated herein are true, as of the date of the electronic filing, in compliance with R.I. Gen. Laws § 7-6.*

By   SYLVIA BERNAL
      Signature of Authorized Person

Form No. 631
Revised 09/07

© 2007 - 2021 State of Rhode Island
All Rights Reserved

RI SOS   Filing Number: 202216257500   Date: 4/29/2022 12:00:00 PM

State of Rhode Island
Office of the Secretary of State

Division Of Business Services
148 W. River Street
Providence RI 02904-2615
(401) 222-3040

Fee: $20.00

Non-Profit Corporation
Annual Report
Filing Period: February 1 - May 1

In accordance with R.I.G.L. 7-6-94, each corporation failing or refusing to file its annual report within the time prescribed by law (R.I.G.L. 7-6-91) is subject to a penalty fee of $25.00.

ANNUAL REPORT YEAR: 2022

1. Corporate ID No. 000125204

2. Name of Corporation RHODE ISLAND LATINO CIVIC FUND

3. State of Incorporation

State: RI

ARTICLE III

Using the dropdown labeled NAICS Code below, select the classification title that describes the primary type of activity in which your entity engages. The box to the right of the dropdown will populate a NAICS Code based on the chosen selection. If the NAICS Code is known, enter it into the box on the right. For further assistance with selecting a classification click here.

NAICS Code
813990

4. Principal Office Address

No. and Street: 26 VERNON ST
City or Town: PROVIDENCE   State: RI   Zip: 02903   Country: USA

5. Brief Description of the Character of the Affairs Conducted in Rhode Island

TO PROMOTE THE PARTICIPATION OF THE LATINO COMMUNITY IN THE CIVIC LIFE AND DEMOCRATIC PROCESSES OF RHODE ISLAND

6. Names and Addresses of the Officers and Directors:

All Directors and Officers must be listed individually. The number of DIRECTORS of a Rhode Island Corporation shall not be less than 3.

Title	Individual Name First, Middle, Last, Suffix	Address Address, City or Town, State, Zip Code, Country
PRESIDENT	MARIBEL ECHEVERRY	87 VARNUM PAWTUCKET, RI 02860 USA

TREASURER	SYLVIA BERNAL	26 VERNONST PROVIDENCE, RI 02903 USA
VICE PRESIDENT	KATYA M RODRIGUEZ ROMAN	63 PITMAN, UNIT 3 PROVIDENCE, RI 02906 USA
DIRECTOR	VICTOR REGINO	56 BLISS EAST PROVIDENCE, RI 02914 USA
DIRECTOR	MARIA CRUZ	90 SAGE DR WARWICK, RI 02886 USA
DIRECTOR	KATYA M RODRIGUEZ ROMAN	63 PITMAN UNIT 3 PROVIDENCE, RI 02906 USA

7. REGISTERED AGENT IN RHODE ISLAND - DO NOT ALTER
Changes Require Filing of Form 641 - R.I.G.L. 7-6-13 / 7-6-78

SYLVIA BERNAL 26 VERNON ST PROVIDENCE , RI 02903

8. This report must be signed by either the President, Vice President, Secretary, Assistant Secretary, Treasurer, duly Authorized Representative, Receiver, or Trustee.

Signed this 29 Day of April, 2022 at 12:03:39 PM by the authorized person. *This electronic signature of the individual or individuals signing this instrument constitutes the affirmation or acknowledgement of the signatory, under penalties of perjury, that this instrument is that individual's act and deed or the act and deed of the company, and that the facts stated herein are true, as of the date of the electronic filing, in compliance with R.I. Gen. Laws § 7-6.*

By SYLVIA BERNAL
Signature of Authorized Person

Form No. 631
Revised 09/07

© 2007 - 2022 State of Rhode Island
All Rights Reserved

RI SOS Filing Number: 202333949320 Date: 4/25/2023 5:27:00 PM

State of Rhode Island
Office of the Secretary of State

Division Of Business Services
148 W. River Street
Providence RI 02904-2615
(401) 222-3040

Fee: $20.00

Non-Profit Corporation
Annual Report
Filing Period: February 1 - May 1

In accordance with R.I.G.L. 7-6-94, each corporation failing or refusing to file its annual report within the time prescribed by law (R.I.G.L. 7-6-91) is subject to a penalty fee of $25.00.

ANNUAL REPORT YEAR - ENTER THE CURRENT FILING YEAR 2023: 2023

1. Corporate ID No. 000125204

2. Name of Corporation RHODE ISLAND LATINO CIVIC FUND

3. State of Incorporation

State: RI

ARTICLE III

Using the dropdown labeled NAICS Code below, select the classification title that describes the primary type of activity in which your entity engages. The box to the right of the dropdown will populate a NAICS Code based on the chosen selection. If the NAICS Code is known, enter it into the box on the right. For further assistance with selecting a classification click here.

NAICS Code
813990

4. Principal Office Address

No. and Street: 26 VERNON ST
City or Town: PROVIDENCE State: RI Zip: 02903 Country: USA

5. Brief Description of the Character of the Affairs Conducted in Rhode Island

TO PROMOTE THE PARTICIPATION OF THE LATINO COMMUNITY IN THE CIVIC LIFE AND DEMOCRATIC PROCESSES OF RHODE ISLAND

6. Names and Addresses of the Officers and Directors:

All Directors and Officers must be listed individually. The number of DIRECTORS of a Rhode Island Corporation shall not be less than 3.

Title	Individual Name	Address

	First, Middle, Last, Suffix	Address, City or Town, State, Zip Code, Country
PRESIDENT	MARIBEL ECHEVERRY	87 VARNUM PAWTUCKET, RI 02860 USA
TREASURER	SYLVIA BERNAL	26 VERNONST PROVIDENCE, RI 02903 USA
SECRETARY	VICTOR REGINO	56 BLISS EAST PROVIDENCE, RI 02914 USA
DIRECTOR	SYLVIA BERNAL	26 VERNON ST PROVIDENCE, RI 02903 USA
DIRECTOR	VICTOR REGINO	56 BLISS EAST PROVIDENCE, RI 02914 USA
DIRECTOR	MARIA CRUZ	90 SAGE DR WARWICK, RI 02886 USA

7. REGISTERED AGENT IN RHODE ISLAND - DO NOT ALTER
Changes Require Filing of Form 641 - R.I.G.L. 7-6-13 / 7-6-78

SYLVIA BERNAL 26 VERNON ST PROVIDENCE , RI 02903

8. This report must be signed by either the President, Vice President, Secretary, Assistant Secretary, Treasurer, duly Authorized Representative, Receiver, or Trustee.

Signed this 25 Day of April, 2023 at 5:31:32 PM by the authorized person. *This electronic signature of the individual or individuals signing this instrument constitutes the affirmation or acknowledgement of the signatory, under penalties of perjury, that this instrument is that individual's act and deed or the act and deed of the company, and that the facts stated herein are true, as of the date of the electronic filing, in compliance with R.I. Gen. Laws § 7-6.*

By SYLVIA BERNAL
    Signature of Authorized Person

Form No. 631
Revised 09/07

© 2007 - 2023 State of Rhode Island
All Rights Reserved

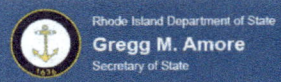

Rhode Island Department of State
Gregg M. Amore
Secretary of State

Business Entity

Name: RHODE ISLAND LATINO CIVIC FUND

Feature not available ☐ check all	Name of filing	Year filed	Date filed	Filing No.	View PDF
☐	Annual Report	2023	04/25/2023 05:27 PM	202333949320	202333949320_1.pdf, 2 pgs
☐	Annual Report	2022	04/29/2022 12:00 PM	202216257500	202216257500_1.pdf, 2 pgs
☐	Annual Report	2021	06/30/2021 10:36 PM	202198883470	202198883470_1.pdf, 2 pgs
☐	Annual Report	2020	07/01/2020 07:12 PM	202043888160	202043888160_1.pdf, 2 pgs
☐	Annual Report	2019	07/25/2019 05:24 PM	201907595150	201907595150_1.pdf, 2 pgs
☐	Annual Report	2018	05/22/2018 10:50 AM	201866637700	201866637700_1.pdf, 1 pgs
☐	Annual Report	2017	05/22/2018 10:49 AM	201866638220	201866638220_1.pdf, 1 pgs
☐	Annual Report	2016	09/12/2016 01:50 PM	201608686300	201608686300_1.pdf, 1 pgs
☐	Annual Report	2015	09/12/2016 01:49 PM	201608686670	201608686670_1.pdf, 1 pgs
☐	Annual Report	2014	06/11/2014 04:00 PM	201440830620	201440830620_1.pdf, 2 pgs
☐	Annual Report	2013	04/08/2014 04:26 PM	201438098250	201438098250_1.pdf, 2 pgs
☐	Annual Report	2012	07/31/2012 10:13 PM	201295489370	201295489370_1.pdf, 3 pgs
☐	Annual Report	2011	02/01/2012 11:05 AM	201288831070	201288831070_1.pdf, 2 pgs
☐	Annual Report	2010	07/08/2010 07:22 AM	201064638770	201064638770_1.pdf, 2 pgs
☐	Annual Report	2009	06/30/2009 10:24 PM	200947904340	200947904340_1.pdf, 3 pgs
☐	Annual Report	2008	06/30/2008 02:43 PM	200812204210	200812204210_1.pdf, 3 pgs
	Annual Report	2007	07/12/2007 12:00 AM		Index Number = None (0 pages)

Business Entity

Name: RHODE ISLAND LATINO CIVIC FUND

Feature not available check all	Name of filing	Year filed	Date filed	Filing No.	View PDF
	Annual Report	2019	07/25/2019 05:24 PM	201907595150	201907595150_1.pdf, 2 pgs
	Statement of Change of Registered/Resident Agent		05/22/2018 10:51 AM	201866635490	201866635490_1.pdf, 1 pgs
	Annual Report	2018	05/22/2018 10:50 AM	201866637700	201866637700_1.pdf, 1 pgs
	Annual Report	2017	05/22/2018 10:49 AM	201866638220	201866638220_1.pdf, 1 pgs
	Reinstatement		05/22/2018 10:48 AM	201866633450	201866633450_1.pdf, 1 pgs
	Revocation Certificate For Failure to File the Annual Report for the Year		04/18/2018 10:18 AM	201862354700	201862354700_1.pdf, 1 pgs
	Revocation Notice For Failure to File An Annual Report		02/02/2018 11:21 AM	201857339480	201857339480_1.pdf, 1 pgs
	Annual Report	2016	09/12/2016 01:50 PM	201608686300	201608686300_1.pdf, 1 pgs
	Annual Report	2015	09/12/2016 01:49 PM	201608686670	201608686670_1.pdf, 1 pgs
	Reinstatement		09/12/2016 01:48 PM	201608686030	201608686030_1.pdf, 1 pgs
	Revocation Certificate For Failure to File the Annual Report for the Year		02/09/2016 12:04 PM	201692169730	201692169730_1.pdf, 1 pgs
	Revocation Notice For Failure to File An Annual Report		11/18/2015 10:25 AM	201587986660	201587986660_1.pdf, 1 pgs
	Statement of Change of Registered/Resident Agent		05/01/2015 07:52 AM	201561326530	201561326530_1.pdf, 2 pgs
	Annual Report	2014	06/11/2014 04:00 PM	201440830620	201440830620_1.pdf, 2 pgs
	Annual Report	2013	04/08/2014 04:26 PM	201438098250	201438098250_1.pdf, 2 pgs
	Reinstatement		04/08/2014 04:25 PM	201438098070	201438098070_1.pdf, 1 pgs
	Revocation Certificate For Failure to File the Annual Report for the Year		03/12/2014 12:08 PM	201437016750	201437016750_1.pdf, 1 pgs
	Revocation Notice For Failure to File An Annual Report		11/14/2013 08:42 AM	201330576090	201330576090_1.pdf, 1 pgs
	Statement of Change of Registered/Resident Agent		05/27/2013 09:51 PM	201321609880	201321609880_1.pdf, 2 pgs
	Statement of Change of Registered/Resident Agent		07/31/2012 10:31 PM	201295489550	201295489550_1.pdf, 2 pgs
	Annual Report	2012	07/31/2012 10:13 PM	201295489370	201295489370_1.pdf, 3 pgs
	Annual Report	2011	02/01/2012 11:05 AM	201288831070	201288831070_1.pdf, 2 pgs
	Revocation Notice For Failure to File An Annual Report		01/31/2012 08:52 AM	201288682780	201288682780_1.pdf, 1 pgs
	Annual Report	2010	07/08/2010 07:22 AM	201064638770	201064638770_1.pdf, 2 pgs
	Statement of Change of Registered/Resident Agent		07/08/2010 07:11 AM	201064638590	201064638590_1.pdf, 2 pgs
	Articles of Amendment		07/08/2010 06:55 AM	201064638400	201064638400_1.pdf, 3 pgs
	Annual Report	2009	06/30/2009 10:24 PM	200947904340	200947904340_1.pdf, 3 pgs
	Annual Report	2008	06/30/2008 02:43 PM	200812204210	200812204210_1.pdf, 3 pgs
	Annual Report	2007	07/12/2007 12:00 AM		Index Number = None (0 pages)
	Statement of Change of Registered/Resident Agent		06/06/2006 12:00 AM	201859294570	201859294570_1.pdf, 1 pgs
	Annual Reports - Prior to 2006	2005	05/24/2006 12:00 AM	201859295540	201859295540_1.pdf, 3 pgs
	Revocation Notice For Failure to File An Annual Report		03/20/2006 11:00 PM	201859294930	201859294930_1.pdf, 1 pgs
	Statement of Change of Registered/Resident Agent		08/16/2004 12:00 AM	201859295720	201859295720_1.pdf, 1 pgs
	Revocation Notice For Failure to File An Annual Report		03/09/2004	201859296060	201859296060_1.pdf, 1 pgs
	Articles of Incorporation		06/11/2002	201859296150	201859296150_1.pdf, 3 pgs

Note:

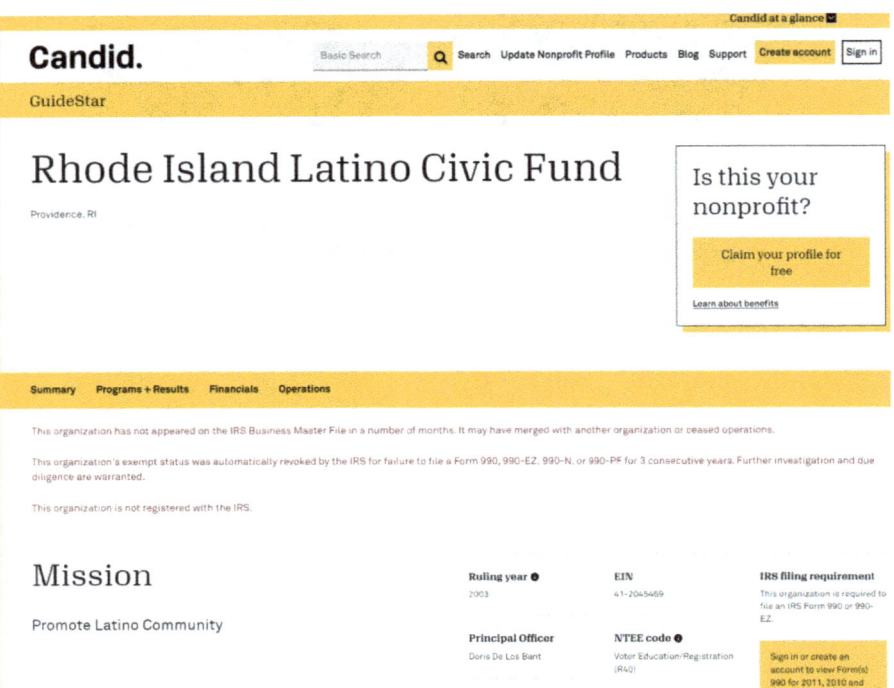

GuideStar

CIVIL RIGHTS, SOCIAL ACTION, ADVOCACY (R)

RHODE ISLAND LATINO CIVIC FUND

QUICK FACTS

 Providence, RI

This organization has not appeared on the IRS Business Master File in a number of months. It may have merged with another organization or ceased operations.

This organization's exempt status was automatically revoked by the IRS for failure to file a Form 990, 990-EZ, 990-N, or 990-PF for 3 consecutive years. Further investigation and due diligence are warranted.

This organization is not registered with the IRS.

| SUMMARY | PROGRAMS + RESULTS | FINANCIALS | OPERATIONS |

Mission

Promote Latino Community

Ruling Year
2003

EIN
41-2045469

Principal Officer
Doris De Los Bant

BRIDGE Number
1358105193

Main Address
PO Box 23020

Providence , RI 02903

Show More Contacts

Cause Area (NTEE Code)

Voter Education/Registration (R40)

IRS Filing Requirement

This organization is required to file an IRS Form 990 or 990-EZ.

Download Tax Forms

Show Forms 990

Roger Williams University deepens ties to Latino community

School of Continuing Studies partners with R.I. Latino Civic Fund

Posted Jul. 14, 2016 at 12:53 PM
Updated Jul 14, 2016 at 3:56 PM

PROVIDENCE — In a development that broadens its reach into diverse local communities, Roger Williams University's School of Continuing Studies on Thursday formally entered into a partnership with the Rhode Island Latino Civic Fund.

The latest in a series of community initiatives by Roger Williams, the new alliance is intended to provide greater education and workforce development opportunities for the state's substantial and increasing Hispanic population.

"The growth of the Latino community is even more noticeable and important in a community the size of Rhode Island, where Latinos are accounting for increasingly larger portions of the state population, local workforce and public schools," said Jose Batista, the fund's president. "As a result of this partnership, Latinos will have a broader network with which to share their talents and to learn new skills in order to build stronger communities."

Roger Williams' president Donald J. Farish said such community alliances reflect the philosophy that the school "is a private institution committed to serving the public good."

And in a multicultural world, Farish said, that means more than providing students merely a traditional model of higher education, one that begins after high-school graduation. He listed some of the more innovative opportunities that the new partnership — and existing ones with the cities of Central Falls and Pawtucket, and other community organizations — provide.

They include programs for "current high-school students interested in earning college credits while still in high school, working adults who want to acquire new knowledge to qualify for better jobs, recent parolees who need life skills to avoid going back to prison, and the economic needs of urban communities."

School of Continuing Studies dean Jamie E. Scurry, who has been instrumental in building the university's community partnerships, said that when she began her work in this area Roger Williams adhered to a longstanding model — one that was effective for some adults, but not necessarily for others.

"The School of Continuing Studies basically served what I would call your traditional adult learner," she said, "somebody who's already on a career pathway, already looking for a degree, and really needs a credential as much as they need to expand their knowledge. As well as active duty-military, a pretty traditional type of adult learning."

Scurry has led a four-year process of determining and meeting community needs — a process, she told The Providence Journal, that began with listening to individuals, community groups, municipalities and businesses.

The central question, she said, was how to develop programs for adults of any age, wherever they live, "no matter where they are on their journey, whether it's their second, third or fourth chance."

he new approach, she said, has transformed the School of Continuing Studies, which has associate's and bachelor's degree programs, along with certificate programs.

"It's a whole different way of thinking," Scurry said. "We can't sort of ride in on a white horse as an institution and say we have the answer. It's tearing down the walls and really saying, 'The community is like our campus. This is how we work together.' "

RWU School of Continuing Studies Formalizes Partnership with Rhode Island Latino Civic Fund

Partnership will provide programs and resources to the State's growing Latino population

At left, José Batista, president of the R.I. Latino Civic Fund, celebrates the new partnership with RWU School of Continuing Studies Dean Jamie Scurry (right) and RWU President Donald J. Farish (center).

By: Public Affairs Staff
July 15, 2016

PROVIDENCE, R.I. – Roger Williams University School of Continuing Studies and the Rhode Island Latino Civic Fund today announced a new partnership that will enhance collaborative opportunities, as well as provide university-supported resources to the RILCF and its efforts to provide inclusive civic education and political participation among the Ocean State's Latino population.

"Roger Williams University is a private institution committed to serving the public good," said Roger Williams University President Donald J. Farish. "Our partnership with the Latino Civic Fund speaks directly to our commitment to expand our innovative adult education initiatives through the School of Continuing Studies to help thousands of Rhode Islanders develop the skills they need to succeed in today's workforce and improve their quality of life."

Going forward, the R.I. Latino Civic Fund will operate out of RWU's new Providence Campus at One Empire Plaza. The colocation will increase synergies between RICLF and the School of Continuing Studies, including programming to be developed around the Latina Leadership Institute – an initiative launched in 2003 that empowers women from all walks of life to sharpen their leadership skills and facilitate community management. There are currently more than 300 LLI alumnae, including prominent community leaders, business owners and elected officials. These graduates will be eligible for discounted tuition on enrollment in School of Continuing Studies programs for the duration of the partnership.

"Through this partnership, Latinos in Rhode Island will now have greater access to higher education, workforce training and community partnerships. The result will be a broader network with which to share their talents and to learn new skills in order to build stronger communities," said José Batista, president of the Latino Civic Fund. "I am grateful to Roger Williams University for taking a leadership role in fostering relationships with the Latino community in Rhode Island. I look forward to working with RWU in the coming years and am confident our partnership will foster growth and progress not only for the Latino community, but for all Rhode Islanders."

The new partnership highlights the School of Continuing Studies' ongoing efforts to remove barriers to education and community development while supporting the needs of multicultural communities with personalized educational and professional development opportunities.

"The School of Continuing Studies is committed to working in collaboration with community- based organizations and municipalities to remove barriers to education and workforce development and help a greater population of individuals take the next steps towards their career goals," said RWU School of Continuing Studies Dean Jamie Scurry. " Through our partnership with the Latino Civic Fund we will work collaboratively to meet the needs of people at all stages in their educational journey – recent high school graduates, current high school students interested in earning college credit and working adults who want to acquire new skills to help them move forward in their careers."

Reference Sources

Tomás Ávila, Latinas @ a Crossroad: Nuestro Political Empowerment, 1999

Honoring the Past, Celebrating the Present & Imagining the Future, 1999

E. Susan Barber with additions by Barbara Orbach Natanson, One Hundred Years toward Suffrage: An Overview

Melba Depeña, Destino 2002

Ana Maria Brasileiro, Women's Leadership in a Changing World: Reflecting on Experience in Latin America and the Caribbean, (New York, NY: UNIFEM, 1996).

William H. Chafe, The American Woman: Her Changing Social, Economic, and Political Roles, 1920-1970.

Linda Chavez, Out of the Barrio : Toward a New Politics of Hispanic Assimilation (New York, Basic Books, 1992).

Nancy Cott, The Grounding of Modern Feminism.

Thomas Dublin, Women at Work: The Transformation of Work and Community in Lowell, Massachusetts, 1826-1860.

Sara M. Evans, Born for Liberty: A History of Women in America.

Eleanor Flexner, Century of Struggle: The Woman's Rights Movement in the United States, rev. ed.

Debra Franklin, The Heritage We Claim: College of Notre Dame of Maryland, 1896- 1996.

Elizabeth Frost-Knappman, The ABC-CLIO Companion to Women's Progress in America.

League of Women Voters of the United States
National American Woman Suffrage Association (NAWSA) Collection, Rare Books Division, Library of Congress, Washington, D.C.

National Hispana Leadership Institute, Follow the Leader: Women's Ways of Mentoring (Denver, CO: 1992).

MassInc, A Discussion of Women In Politics, 1990

Carol Hardy-Fafa,, Latina Politics, Latino Politics: Gender, Culture, and Political Participation in Boston, Temple University Press, Philadelphia, 1993,

RILPAC, Women's Suffrage 80th Anniversary Celebration, August 31, 2000

Ruth Rosen, The 20th Century's Longest Revolution Still Has Work to Do
Women now matter and society has been transformed; the next generation must assume the mantle. 1999

Anne Firor Scott and Andrew Scott, One Half the People: The Fight for Woman Suffrage; "From Parlor to Politics," permanent exhibit at the Museum of American History, Smithsonian Institution, Washington, D.C.

Dorothy Sterling, ed. We Are Your Sisters: Black Women in the Nineteenth Century.

Marjorie Spruill Wheeler, The History of the Suffrage Movement by

Zophy, Angela Howard and Frances M. Kavenik, eds. Handbook of American Women's History.

Report of the Woman's Right, Held at SENECA FALLS, N.Y., July 19th and 20th, 1848. ROCHESTER: Printed by John Dick, at the North Star Office.

www.ingramcontent.com/pod-product-compliance
Lightning Source LLC
Chambersburg PA
CBHW050835230426
43667CB00012B/2009